Ontology-Based Interpretation of Natural Language

Synthesis Lectures on Human Language Technologies

Editor
Graeme Hirst, *University of Toronto*

Synthesis Lectures on Human Language Technologies is edited by Graeme Hirst of the University of Toronto. The series consists of 50- to 150-page monographs on topics relating to natural language processing, computational linguistics, information retrieval, and spoken language understanding. Emphasis is on important new techniques, on new applications, and on topics that combine two or more HLT subfields.

Ontology-Based Interpretation of Natural Language
Philipp Cimiano, Christina Unger, and John McCrae
2014

Web Corpus Construction
Roland Schäfer and Felix Bildhauer
2013

Recognizing Textual Entailment: Models and Applications
Ido Dagan, Dan Roth, Mark Sammons, and Fabio Massimo Zanzotto
2013

Linguistic Fundamentals for Natural Language Processing: 100 Essentials from Morphology and Syntax
Emily M. Bender
2013

Semi-Supervised Learning and Domain Adaptation in Natural Language Processing
Anders Søgaard
2013

Semantic Relations Between Nominals
Vivi Nastase, Preslav Nakov, Diarmuid Ó Séaghdha, and Stan Szpakowicz
2013

Computational Modeling of Narrative
Inderjeet Mani
2012

v

Spoken Dialogue Systems
Kristiina Jokinen and Michael McTear
2009

Introduction to Chinese Natural Language Processing
Kam-Fai Wong, Wenjie Li, Ruifeng Xu, and Zheng-sheng Zhang
2009

Introduction to Linguistic Annotation and Text Analytics
Graham Wilcock
2009

Dependency Parsing
Sandra Kübler, Ryan McDonald, and Joakim Nivre
2009

Statistical Language Models for Information Retrieval
ChengXiang Zhai
2008

Ontology-Based Interpretation of Natural Language

Philipp Cimiano, Christina Unger, and John McCrae

ISBN: 978-3-031-01026-2   paperback
ISBN: 978-3-031-02154-1   ebook

DOI 10.1007/978-3-031-02154-1

A Publication in Springer Publishers series
SYNTHESIS LECTURES ON HUMAN LANGUAGE TECHNOLOGIES

Lecture #24
Series Editor: Graeme Hirst, *University of Toronto*
Series ISSN
Print 1947-4040   Electronic 1947-4059

Ontology-Based Interpretation of Natural Language

Philipp Cimiano, Christina Unger, and John McCrae
Semantic Computing Group
CITEC, Bielefeld University

SYNTHESIS LECTURES ON HUMAN LANGUAGE TECHNOLOGIES #24

ABSTRACT

For humans, understanding a natural language sentence or discourse is so effortless that we hardly ever think about it. For machines, however, the task of interpreting natural language, especially grasping meaning beyond the literal content, has proven extremely difficult and requires a large amount of background knowledge. This book focuses on the interpretation of natural language with respect to specific domain knowledge captured in ontologies. The main contribution is an approach that puts ontologies at the center of the interpretation process. This means that ontologies not only provide a formalization of domain knowledge necessary for interpretation but also support and guide the construction of meaning representations.

We start with an introduction to ontologies and demonstrate how linguistic information can be attached to them by means of the ontology lexicon model *lemon*. These lexica then serve as basis for the automatic generation of grammars, which we use to compositionally construct meaning representations that conform with the vocabulary of an underlying ontology. As a result, the level of representational granularity is not driven by language but by the semantic distinctions made in the underlying ontology and thus by distinctions that are relevant in the context of a particular domain. We highlight some of the challenges involved in the construction of ontology-based meaning representations, and show how ontologies can be exploited for ambiguity resolution and the interpretation of temporal expressions. Finally, we present a question answering system that combines all tools and techniques introduced throughout the book in a real-world application, and sketch how the presented approach can scale to larger, multi-domain scenarios in the context of the Semantic Web.

KEYWORDS

natural language processing, ontologies, ontology lexica, grammar generation, ambiguity resolution, temporal interpretation, question answering, Semantic Web

Contents

List of Figures

Preface

The semantic interpretation of natural language text constitutes the holy grail for computational linguistics. Interpreting a sentence does not only mean to capture its propositional content but also requires ontological axioms that support the inference of additional meaning implications that the sentence has beyond what is explicitly expressed. If we ever want to reach this holy grail, we need to understand better in which formalisms such ontological axioms can be encoded and how they can be leveraged to guide and constrain the interpretation process. However, in recent years not too much sleep has been lost in the community on how to do this. This is surprising given that the amount of knowledge published on the web as part of the Semantic Web initiative has been steadily growing. Further, the Semantic Web community has spent great efforts in providing standardized frameworks for the representation, publication and sharing of ontological knowledge on the web, developing widely accepted standards which, however, have largely gone unnoticed in the computational semantics field.

This book aims to bring together traditional approaches to semantic interpretation of natural language text and recent developments in the Semantic Web field, attempting to provide a step toward a synergy between these two fields that have so far remained rather separate from each other. To this end, we will present a principled approach to exploit ontologies for the purpose of natural language interpretation. In particular, this book summarizes the main results of research on two topics that have been at the heart of our agenda for several years and drove many of our investigations. The first one is ontology lexicalization, i.e., the enrichment of ontologies with extensive linguistic information, which manifested in the development of a model for ontology lexica. The second one is the exploitation of such information for the interpretation of natural language. We explored how ontology lexica can serve as basis for the automatic generation of grammars, how these grammars can be used for the construction of meaning representations that conform with the vocabulary and structure of an underlying ontology, and how a resulting ontology-based interpretation process can be part of applications like domain-specific question answering over Semantic Web data.

The book introduces our approach to natural language interpretation that puts ontologies in the center of the interpretation process, demonstrates how such an approach can be put to work and highlights its potentials and challenges. The material included is based on a course that we gave at the European Summer School in Logic, Language and Information (ESSLLI) in 2012 and at Bielefeld University.

Our approach still needs to be shown to robustly scale to larger, non-trivial amounts of texts and discourses. However, the main tenets of the approach we present are still valid in spite of this outstanding proof of concept. We are convinced that domain-specific ontology axioms—whether acquired or hand-coded—are a crucial ingredient for any semantic interpretation approach that aims to go beyond the purely propositional content of natural language sentences. Without ontological knowledge on which to reason upon, we will be limited to grasping only the superficial meaning of a natural language at best. We hope that this book thus also stimulates other researchers to look into the problem of how to unveil the deeper semantic content of a sentence. If somebody finds a way to do so, circumventing the need for axiomatic ontological knowledge, we will bow humbly.

TARGET AUDIENCE AND PREREQUISITES

This book is targeted at researchers from natural language processing interested in deep language processing with respect to a conceptual formalization of a domain, researchers from the Semantic Web community interested in methods and tools for language-based interfaces to structured data, and researchers from linguistics interested in the application of linguistic theories in the context of the automatic construction of meaning representations. We provide exercises, so the book can be used both for self study and as a basis for teaching.

Throughout the book, we assume a basic familiarity with first-order logic. If you need a refresher, The *Handbook of Philosophical Logic,* edited by Dov M. Gabbay and Franz Guenthner, provides an excellent starting point, guide and reference. If you prefer a gentle introduction with lots of philosophical background and remarks, we recommend Hodges [2001]. For an introduction to logic for computer science, see e.g. Genesereth and Kao [2013], and for an introduction targeted at linguists, see Gamut [1991].

In addition, Chapters 4–6 and 9 assume basic knowledge of Semantic Web languages, especially RDF. Section 1.4 of the introduction provides a crash course in RDF that summarizes everything needed for the rest of the book and provides some pointers for further reading and reference. Readers who are fluent in Turtle RDF can safely skip this section.

All examples in this book will come from the soccer domain. We decided on soccer as it offers the right level of complexity in language and ontology, being restricted enough but being far away from trivial. If soccer played no role in your life so far, Section 1.5 of the introduction provides you with everything you need to know to enjoy the examples in this book. Again, if you already know what penalty kick and offside means, you can skip this section.

STRUCTURE OF THE BOOK

The first chapters provide the background on ontologies, lexica and linguistic formalisms on which we build. After illustrating the process of constructing ontology-specific semantic representations, subsequent chapters then explore how reasoning can support this process, how it can be extended and finally how it can be used in a specific application.

Chapter 2 gives an introduction to ontologies, showing how knowledge can be modeled in different formalisms ranging from first-order logic to various flavors of description logics, with a particular consideration of the OWL and OWL 2 standards. We will pick soccer as the underlying domain of the examples throughout the book, and at the end of the chapter the reader will be equipped with a basic formal conceptualization of that domain.

Chapter 3 introduces the linguistic formalisms that this book uses. The grammars we create and use build on *Lexicalized Tree Adjoining Grammars* for syntactic representations and on *Underspecified Discourse Representation Theory*, in particular on a notational variant called DUDES, for semantic representations. We will see how the structure and meaning of words and sentences are captured in these formalisms, and how they can be composed.

Chapter 4 describes the lexicon ontology model *lemon*, a declarative model of the lexicon-ontology interface that allows defining how the concepts defined in an ontology are realized linguistically.

Chapter 5 discusses an approach to automatically generate grammars from *lemon* lexica, thus reducing the cost involved in developing domain-specific grammars.

Chapter 6 illustrates the process of constructing semantic representations within our example domain by means of specific examples, demonstrating some of the challenges one encounters in this process.

Chapter 7 discusses the interaction between the process of interpretation and reasoning, focusing in particular on the case of using ontological restrictions to reduce the number of readings of a natural language sentence.

Chapter 8 presents a theory for temporal interpretation that is based on the *time ontology*, as one example of a module crucial for the interpretation of natural language that is domain-independent and thus reusable across domains and applications.

Chapter 9 presents an instantiation of our approach for the case of a question answering system over RDF data. It thereby demonstrates how our approach can be used in a specific application.

Chapter 10 then summarizes the main vision behind this book and provides an outlook on future developments.

RESOURCES

All material accompanying the book, such as the example ontology and lexicon we use as well as pointers to implementations, is available on the book website:

http://www.ontosem.net/book/

Philipp Cimiano, Christina Unger, and John McCrae
January 2014

Acknowledgments

We acknowledge support by the European Commission through the projects Monnet (FP7-248458) and PortDial (FP7-296170), by which some of the results described in this book have been funded, as well as support from the Deutsche Forschungsgemeinschaft (DFG) through the Excellence Center *Cognitive Interaction Technology* (CITEC). We also thank all our colleagues and students that have provided feedback on lectures and other material that have ultimately found their culmination in this book.

Philipp Cimiano, Christina Unger, and John McCrae
January 2014

CHAPTER 1

Introduction

As humans, understanding a sentence or utterance that we hear or read is so effortless that we hardly ever think consciously about what it means to *understand* a sentence and how we accomplish this task. Take the following description of a soccer game as an example:

1. Right after Puskás's early opening goal, Hungary extended its lead. But the Germans soon drew level, and a long-range shot by Rahn finally determined Germany's surprising victory.

Being familiar with the occurring expressions, we have no trouble in imagining situations that are described. For example, such a situation witnessed five goals. The first one was scored by Puskás and if you are familiar with soccer, you know that it probably happened within the first 10 or 15 minutes of the game, as it otherwise would not count as early. Further we understand that it was followed by another goal raising the score to 2-0 (or 0-2) in favor of Hungary and three subsequent goals for Germany, two equalizing the score to 2-2 and one raising it to 2-3 (or 3-2), although none of those goals is mentioned explicitly. In addition, we perform a number of default inferences, e.g., assuming that Puskás played for Hungary and Rahn played for Germany. Such default inferences can, however, be overridden, for example learning that one of the goals was an own goal.

As humans, we thus grasp a lot of meaning that goes beyond the literal content of the sentence, and we have no problem in inferring the conditions that have to be met by any situation that a sentence can be said to describe.

The task of understanding a natural language sentence or discourse can thus in essence be seen as identifying possible situations that the sentence in question might describe. As easy and effortless as this task is for humans, it is extremely difficult for machines, and no approach exists to date that can robustly interpret language as humans do. In many cases, the understood meaning of a natural language sentence or utterance contains a lot of implicit pieces that need to be brought to the surface. What allows us humans to understand implicit and inferred content of sentences and utterances is the fact that we possess a lot of background knowledge about the world in which we live. This knowledge allows us to draw all kinds of semantic and pragmatic inferences, which then guide our interpretation process. Take the following small discourse as example:

2. After Australia had won 31-0, the coach criticized the World Cup qualification format. He suggested it should avoid such unbalanced games.

In the first sentence, we understand that Australia refers not to the country but to their soccer team, on the basis of the provided context. Further, we understand that the coach mentioned in the first sentence of 2 most probably is the one of the Australian team, due to our knowledge about soccer, comprising the fact that every team has a coach. Additionally, the interplay of world and linguistic knowledge allows us to resolve the pronoun he in the second sentence to that same coach, as no other entity mentioned in the discourse is a person, while we interpret the pronoun it to refer to the qualification format.

For the purpose of allowing a machine or computer program to also draw such inferences and thus understand natural language beyond the mere explicitly expressed content of the sentence, a large amount of background knowledge is needed. And a crucial question is where this knowledge comes from. While there have been some projects attempting to capture and axiomatize common sense human knowledge with a very broad scope, such as *Cyc*[1] or the *Common Sense Computing Initiative*,[2] it is unlikely that there will ever exist one single monolithic source of world knowledge that will contain all the knowledge relevant for natural language interpretation and reasoning. Intuitively, acquiring and modeling the knowledge required to interpret language in a well-circumscribed domain will be much easier and more feasible than encoding all the knowledge necessary to interpret arbitrary language input. In this book we will therefore focus on the interpretation of natural language with respect to a particular domain, hinting at how this approach can scale to larger, multi-domain scenarios in the context of the Semantic Web.

In order to interpret natural language sentences with respect to domain knowledge, a machine needs:

- a formalization of the domain knowledge,

- a process for building meaning representations that are aligned to that domain knowledge, and

- a way to draw inferences and use the resulting information in the interpretation process.

The goal of this book is to present an approach that offers instantiations of these three points by exploiting ontologies. Ontologies not only provide formalizations of domain knowledge but can also support and guide the interpretation process.

1.1   ONTOLOGY-BASED INTERPRETATION OF NATURAL LANGUAGE

Our approach to ontology-based interpretation of natural language puts an ontology at the center of the interpretation process, in order to scope and guide that process in a principled fashion. In this line, the level of representational granularity at which the meaning of natural language is captured is not driven by language, but by the semantic distinctions made in an ontology and thus by distinctions that are relevant in the context of a particular domain. This is a crucial difference

[1]http://www.cyc.com/
[2]http://csc.media.mit.edu/

to extant paradigms to meaning construction in natural language, for which an interpretation that conforms with the vocabulary of a given ontology is only an afterthought.

Our approach to ontology-based interpretation of natural language is illustrated in Figure 1.1. It assumes that there is an ontology or set of ontologies with respect to which natural language input will be interpreted. This set of ontologies will be a mix of domain-independent, domain-dependent, task-specific and application-specific ontologies that have been designed independently of the NLP system by some ontology engineer in interaction with domain experts.

Figure 1.1: Approach to ontology-based interpretation of natural language.

Further, we assume that for every ontology there are one or many lexica specifying how the concepts defined in the ontology, i.e., entities, classes and relations, are verbalized in a particular natural language. We call such a lexicon an *ontology lexicon* [Cimiano et al., 2013]. We assume that a lexicon engineer who is familiar with the ontology and the domain in question creates this lexicon for that particular ontology, ideally with the support of some semi-automatic methods (see, e.g., Walter et al. [2013]).

The grammars that are used by the system to interpret natural language in the context of a given ontology are then to a great extent generated automatically from the ontology lexicon. These grammars rely on a vocabulary aligned to the ontology and contain both syntactic and semantic information that is crucial for the compositional process of constructing the meaning of a particular sentence with respect to that given ontology.

The main advantage of introducing a lexical level between the conceptualization and the grammar is to capture the lexical aspects in a formalism-independent way. While some basic understanding of linguistics and lexical semantics is needed for creating a lexicon, the lexicon engineer does not require knowledge about specific grammar formalisms nor about computational or formal semantics and in particular no knowledge about how semantic representations are composed with each other. This also facilitates the exchange of grammar formalisms in case this is desired.

The domain-specific grammars generated from the lexicon will be used together with other grammar modules capturing the meaning of lexical entries that are domain-independent, such as closed-class words including determiners, pronouns, auxiliary verbs, etc. We assume that additional grammar modules are available, including ones for temporal expressions, modality, and so on. The actual interpretation of a natural language utterance is then carried out by using all relevant grammar modules (domain-dependent and ontology-specific as well as domain-independent) and by exploiting the background knowledge in the ontology via a reasoner. Finally, there is some application that builds on the interpretation component, such as a question answering system that computes answers to a user question once that question has been interpreted with respect to the vocabulary of the ontology.

We thus propose a highly modular approach in which the creation of an ontology, a corresponding lexicon, and domain-independent grammar parts proceed independently of each other in the sense that different actors with different expertise are involved in each of these processes and the creation of these resources can be modularized. Clearly, the lexicon creation step requires an ontology as input, but the lexicon can be created independently in the sense that it will not require changes to the ontology. Of course, the ontology can change, in which case the lexicon will have to be extended and adapted. The domain-independent grammar modules for time, modality, etc., will be developed completely independently by experienced grammar engineers and knowledge representation experts. By this modularity and clear separation of subtasks and roles, the hope is that the complexity of creating and maintaining a system can be tamed, and also that the sharing and reuse of ontologies, lexica, and grammars across applications and systems can be facilitated.

The ontology-based approach to natural language interpretation that we advocate here is directly inspired and informed by the *Ontological Semantics* approach [Nirenburg and Raskin, 2004]. We agree with Nirenburg and Raskin in that there is no semantic interpretation without committing to a particular ontology. We also share with their framework the premise that the ontology should be at the center of any approach to natural language interpretation, in the sense that the ontology scopes and guides the very process of interpretation, fixing the type, structure and granularity of the semantic representations constructed. All knowledge resources, such as lexica and grammars, are aligned to the ontology and have the goal of facilitating the construction of ontology-specific semantic representations. Furthermore, our modular approach is in line with the microtheory-based approach of *Ontological Semantics*.

In contrast to the framework of *Ontological Semantics*, in our approach we emphasize the following aspects:

No ontology fits all purposes: We emphasize the fact that the ontology or set of ontologies that the system uses to interpret natural language is in principle replaceable and that there is no single ontology that will be used by the system. While this is not excluded in principle in the *Ontological Semantics* approach, the implementation seems to be specific for a given ontology. Instead, our implementation of *Ontological Semantics* makes it easy to replace the ontology and lexica and thus adapt the interpretation to any domain or application.

Modularity: Having an ecosystem of knowledge resources in mind, our approach supports the reuse of ontologies as well as lexica and grammars for multiple languages. Also, since our approach clearly separates domain grammar modules (generated automatically from an ontology lexicon) and domain-independent grammar modules, the latter become reusable across domains and applications.

Open standards: Nirenburg and Raskin develop their own ontology formalisms, axiomatization of ontologies and reasoning procedures. We think that proprietary formalisms should strongly be avoided and therefore follow existing open standards for the representation of ontologies and ontology lexica. This allows implementations of our approach for example to replace the reasoner at any time, as the interface to other components will be the same.

Ease of use: Ultimately, our goal is to allow non-experts to adopt our framework to create natural language-based applications for their domain and ontology, not requiring linguistic expertise. They merely need to be able to create ontology lexica from which the ontology-specific grammars that drive the behavior of the system will be generated automatically.

Besides emphasizing modularity and replaceability, our approach is a pragmatic one in that we assume that natural language interpretation has to work with the ontologies that exist today, accepting and dealing with their deficiencies rather than waiting for the ontologies of tomorrow that might be produced according to linguistic principles in order to facilitate the task of exploiting them for the purpose of natural language interpretation. Our main contribution is thus to spell out how the idea behind the *Ontological Semantics* framework is instantiated with respect to current state-of-the-art knowledge representation formalisms as well as standards for the representation of the lexicon-ontology interface.

The focus of the book is certainly not on robustness or coverage. Our concern is to emphasize that we need ontology-aligned semantic representations for the purposes of ambiguity reduction, inferencing, and the like. Our goal is to describe a principled approach to arriving at such representations, which could then later be shown to scale by incorporating statistical and machine-learning-based techniques.

In the next section we will briefly review the current state of the art in *natural language processing* (NLP). This will be quite rough and incomplete, glossing over many details and important activities. Its main purpose is to illustrate what can already be done and to highlight the lack of principled and holistic approaches to the interpretation of natural language with respect to domain ontologies.

1.2   STATE OF THE ART IN NATURAL LANGUAGE PROCESSING

Since the so-called statistical turn in the early 1990s [Manning and Schütze, 1999], the focus of the NLP community has been on developing statistical and corpus-based techniques for subtasks such as part-of-speech tagging (the task of assigning a syntactic category to each word in a sentence), named entity recognition (the task of recognizing sequences of tokens referring to an entity with a name), parsing (computing a representation of the syntactic structure of a sentence), etc., while certainly neglecting aspects of semantics and inference (see Nirenburg and Raskin [2004] on this issue). An important research direction is that of supervised and unsupervised word disambiguation, i.e., deciding which meaning—usually from a fixed set of meaning or senses—a particular word in a sentence has [Navigli, 2009]. Another important task that has received a lot of attention is the one on recognizing textual entailments, i.e., of computing the logical relation between two sentences, e.g., whether they entail or contradict each other [Dagan et al., 2009]. While both tasks are clearly important, they are symptomatic of the reductionist attempt of isolating particular aspects of the interpretation of natural language while losing sight of the actual problem of coming up with a proper interpretation of a natural language sentence or discourse as a whole. On the one hand, the task of determining the meaning of words should clearly be one essential aspect of the process of compositionally computing the meaning of a whole sentence, falling out of it thus as a byproduct. Also, isolating the problem of disambiguating the meaning of single words might come with more difficulties and upper performance bounds compared to tackling the problem from a more holistic perspective. On the other hand, textual entailment focuses mainly on drawing inferences with knowledge-lean methods, sidestepping the task of computing an interpretation of a sentence. Background knowledge is thus hidden in procedures that compute some aspect of meaning, but this knowledge is not modeled declaratively and is thus not accessible across all components. This fosters duplication of effort and might also lead to local optima.

Finally, there has also been a lot of work on inducing knowledge from text corpora, an activity that has also been called *ontology learning* [Cimiano, 2006]. There has been a lot of work in this direction, in particular on exploiting distributional similarity to induce synonyms [Yamada et al., 2009], semantically related words [Grefenstette, 1992; Herdagdelen et al., 2009], hyper-nyms, etc. In general, there has been a lot of work on representing the meaning of words using (distributional) vector space models [Erk, 2012]. More recently, such vector space models have been extended to account for compositional interpretation, e.g., of noun compounds [Mitchell and Lapata, 2008] (see Baroni et al. [forthcoming] for research program for vector-based compositional semantics).

A particularly interesting recent research line is the one of *semantic parsing* [Ge and Mooney, 2006; Kate and Mooney, 2006; Wong and Mooney, 2007; Zettlemoyer and Collins, 2005] which is concerned with automatically inducing models that can map natural language input into logical form on the basis of a given set of training examples consisting of natural language input together with the expected logical form. This work is particularly relevant in our context as such approaches could be used to induce a model that maps natural language input into an appropriate ontology-conform representation on the basis of appropriate training data. In any case, while this circumvents the need to define a compositional syntax-semantics interface as described in Chapter 6, it clearly does not circumvent the need for an ontology and semantic representations aligned to it, as we argue for in this book.

With respect to automatically computing a semantic representation of a natural language sentence, current approaches also sidestep the problem of actually interpreting a sentence. Boxer [Curran et al., 2007], one of the most sophisticated such tools, limits itself to computing one logical form that mirrors the syntactic dependencies in the original sentence. The semantic representation computed by Boxer for the sentence in 3a, for example, based on our example in 1, corresponds to the slightly simplified first-order logical representation in 3b.

3. (a) An early opening goal by Puskás put Hungary in the lead.

   (b) $\exists x_0, x_1, x_2$ (event$(x_0) \wedge$ put_in_lead$(x_0) \wedge$
       agent$(x_0, x_1) \wedge$ opening_goal$(x_1) \wedge$ early$(x_1) \wedge$ by$(x_1,$ Puskás$) \wedge$
       patient$(x_0,$ Hungary$))$

Boxer is without doubt a great tool and it performs very robustly on varied input. However, a representation such as the one that Boxer generates is a representation only of the explicit content of the sentence, more specifically of *who does what to whom (why, when, where, and with what)*, that mirrors the syntactic dependency structure. Such a representation is only the first step in the process of semantic interpretation. Without any additional background knowledge that constrains the process of interpretation, such a representation still holds in too many situations. Our understanding of what an opening goal is and what early in the context of a soccer game means are not captured in the above logical representation. So although we can infer that after Puskás's goal the score is 1-0 in favor of Hungary, this inference cannot be drawn on the basis of the logical representation alone.

Computational linguists and semanticists will argue that this is why we need *meaning postulates* (a notion due to Carnap [1947]), which axiomatize the meaning of words, relating them to each other. This is exactly the role that ontologies will play in our approach. But meaning postulates alone do not solve the problem, as we also need an approach to model how they play together with the semantic interpretation process in order to constrain the interpretation of the meaning representation appropriately.

Besides providing us with background knowledge necessary for drawing inferences, ontologies play another very important role: that of a normalizing vocabulary. Since the representations Boxer builds do not rely on any normalizing vocabulary, the semantic representations of sentences which express a very similar meaning can be completely unrelated. Consider the sentence in 4a. Its Boxer representation corresponds to the following slightly simplified first-order logical representation in 4b.

4. (a) Maradona opened the scoring with a goal for Argentina shortly after kick off.

(b) $\exists x_0, x_1, x_2, x_3 \, (\text{event}(x_0) \wedge \text{open}(x_0) \wedge$
$\text{agent}(x_0, \text{Maradona}) \wedge$
$\text{patient}(x_0, x_1) \wedge \text{score}(x_1) \wedge$
$\text{with}(x_0, x_2) \wedge \text{goal}(x_2) \wedge \text{for}(x_2, \text{Argentina}) \wedge$
$\text{shortly\_after}(x_0, x_3) \wedge \text{kick\_off}(x_3))$

While both sentences, 3a and 4a, talk about very similar situations, namely an early first goal that puts one of the teams in the lead, their semantic representations have little in common, as they use completely different vocabulary. For example, in 3b, the scoring player is related to the goal by means of the predicate by, while in 4b, he is related to the event as agent and only the event is related to the goal. Furthermore, in order to draw the same inferences from both sentences, we would need meaning postulates for every word or lemma. For example, the representation in 3b specifies the goal as being early, while the representation in 4b talks about an event shortly_after something that is a kick_off. In order to capture the interpretation that the goal was within the first 10 or 15 minutes, we would need two meaning postulates, one for early and one for shortly_after something that is a kick_off. With a normalizing vocabulary, on the other hand, we would specify meaning postulates for every concept and then map several words to the same concept.

In order to go beyond the *who does what to whom* analysis, we will rely on an ontology specifying the relevant concepts, relations and entities in the domain as a basis to compute semantic representations aligned with this ontological vocabulary, using knowledge axiomatized in the ontology to generate only valid interpretations of the sentence (or discourse) in question.

While Boxer and other state-of-the-art tools for semantic construction realize a crucial first step toward interpreting a natural language sentence, i.e., the computation of a logical form that a machine is able to handle, many textbooks and approaches in the area of NLP often suggest that the final goal of semantic interpretation is to produce such a logical form. We would like to stress that this is only one ingredient in the process of interpreting a natural language sentence. An equally important ingredient—albeit one that is often ignored—is the availability of appropriate domain knowledge in order to constrain the interpretation process to yield only valid interpretations of a sentence and to enrich those interpretations with further inferred content.

1.3   RELATION TO THE SEMANTIC WEB

The Semantic Web vision [Berners-Lee et al., 2001] corresponds to one where content on the web is published in a machine-understandable and formally interpretable fashion so that autonomous agents can discover relevant content, reason on its basis and take appropriate decisions. The Semantic Web vision thus crucially builds on ontologies as formal vocabularies to make the meaning of content explicit in such a way that machines can reason upon it. Citing Berners-Lee et al. [2001], the Semantic Web vision can be described in a nutshell as follows:

> *The Semantic Web is an extension of the current web in which information is given well-defined meaning, better enabling computers and people to work in cooperation.*

While the paper outlines a vision of agents performing planning and decision making to support humans, its authors have often stressed that the goal of the Semantic Web is not to develop intelligent systems that act, but rather to provide the technical infrastructure for the development of such intelligent programs. Since the term and vision of the Semantic Web has been coined in this sense, many research groups worldwide have contributed to the effort of standardizing ontology languages and data models for capturing machine-readable knowledge, as well as on providing the infrastructure for publishing machine-readable data on the web. In particular, the *Web Ontology Language* (or OWL for short) was developed to axiomatize the meaning of symbols we use in describing information by using fragments of first-order logic, in particular description logics. OWL is now an official recommendation by the World Wide Web Consortium (W3C) [McGuinness and van Harmelen, 2004]. Further, the research community has developed a data model for representing data on the web building on triples of the form $(subject, predicate, object)$ as well as query languages to query this body of knowledge. This effort has naturally lead to the *linked data* vision, the central idea of which is to publish data in such a way that it is uniquely referenceable and de-referenceable using standard web protocols and that it builds on existing standards (such as the so-called Resource Description Framework (RDF) [Manola and Miller, 2004] and the RDF query language SPARQL [Prud'hommeaux and Seaborne, 2008]) to facilitate querying and interoperability.

Thus, one undoubtedly great achievement of the Semantic Web community is that it has managed to reach enough consensus to develop standardized knowledge representation formalisms and data models for publishing machine-readable knowledge on the web. This is important as standardization is crucial for industrial adoption and creates incentives for people to develop tools that work with those standards, thus creating an ecosystem of tools and software systems that can be readily used. This in turn has led to many resources being published on the web using the RDF data model and following the so-called linked data principles[3] introduced by Tim Berners-Lee.

In stark contrast to the success story of the Semantic Web, it is indeed amazing how little attention the natural language processing community has been paying to the Semantic Web ini-

---

[3]http://www.w3.org/DesignIssues/LinkedData.html

tiative. The weaknesses of Semantic Web representation formalisms from the NLP point of view are obvious, as it is unclear how one would represent scope, modality, plurals, tense, etc., using Semantic Web formalisms. Nevertheless, by now there are many domain ontologies and datasets out there on the web that could be leveraged for the purposes of natural language interpretation and disambiguation. In fact, as the Semantic Web formalisms have by now the status of standards, there is a plethora of tools, APIs, and reasoners that the NLP community could exploit.

In the instantiation of our approach to ontology-based interpretation of natural language, we heavily build on Semantic Web formalisms, in particular OWL, RDF, and SPARQL. On the one hand, this is a very pragmatic choice as it avoids duplication of effort and allows for building on an existing and mature ecosystem of formalisms and tools. On the other hand, we do not adopt the view of a single NLP system or application but envision an ecosystem of ontological resources that all NLP systems can reuse. Our vision is one where ontologies on the web are enriched with information about how concepts are expressed in different languages by way of publicly available ontology lexica. Such an ecosystem of ontologies and lexical resources would provide the basis for the development of knowledge-based and knowledge-driven NLP applications that build on this growing body of resources as much as possible.

There is already a growing interest in using linked data to represent language resources. This has led in recent years to the emergence of the *Linguistic Linked Open Data (LLOD) cloud*,[4] including different language versions of DBpedia[5] (e.g., English, Spanish, French, Japanese and Russian), a cross-domain knowledge base comprising structured information extracted from Wikipedia infoboxes, the World Atlas of Language Structures (WALS) and lexical resources such as Wiktionary, WordNet and FrameNet. The advantages of linked data for linguistics are (see Chiarcos et al. [2013] on this issue):

Representational adequacy: Linked data primarily uses RDF as representation format, which corresponds to a labeled directed graph. It has been argued by several authors [Bird and Liberman, 2001; Carletta et al., 2005] that this forms a sounder basis for representing language data than tree-based (e.g., XML) or feature-based representation formats.

Structural interoperability: The use of a single data model based on globally unique identifiers allows data to easily be combined by tools and databases.

Federation: The representation of data on the web allows data to be used without first collecting it on a single machine. Instead, data can easily be accessed from remote machines and automatically federated.

Ecosystem: Linked data has seen adoption in many other fields such as bio-medicine and as such there exists a rich set of tools and general-purpose models that can be applied to RDF resources.

---

[4]http://linguistics.okfn.org/llod
[5]http://dbpedia.org

Expressivity: In addition to RDF, the RDF schema vocabulary and OWL ontology language can be used to impose logical constraints on the data so that a reasoner can check the internal consistency of the data.

Conceptual interoperability: The use of linked global identifiers to describe linguistic categories may significantly ease the effort of semantically aligning resources. For example, two resources may use different systems of linguistic categories, but if two repositories for these category systems provide links to one another, data integration is facilitated.

Dynamicity: By importing other resources via links, importing resources are always up-to-date, always referencing the current version of the data. This dynamicity also allows for the correction and expansion of resources without breaking dependencies. However, dynamicity can also be problematic, e.g., in the case where resources change considerably or even become unavailable.

Keeping these advantages in mind, this book attempts to bring us a step forward by instantiating our approach to ontology-based interpretation of natural language with respect to existing Semantic Web standards and formalisms.

1.4   WHAT YOU NEED TO KNOW ABOUT RDF

Information on the Semantic Web is most commonly represented using the *Resource Description Framework* (RDF) [Manola and Miller, 2004], a data model for describing resources on the web in a structured manner. Resources are, to put it simply, everything that can be identified on the web, such as your hometown and its soccer team, all soccer players and matches and tournaments, and so on. RDF uses *Uniform Resource Identifiers* (URIs) to talk about resources. The URI http://dbpedia.org/resource/Pelé, for example, is an identifier for the resource representing the soccer player Pelé; you can type it in a browser and you will get information about that resource.

The RDF data model is essentially a graph consisting of triples of the general form (*subject, predicate, object*), where *subject, predicate* and *object* can be three kinds of nodes: a URI representing an entity defined on the web, a *blank node* representing an anonymous node in a single document (we will give an example later on) or a *literal* for textual, numeric or other forms of serialized data. In Turtle syntax, a format for the terse representation of triples in RDF (see Beckett and Berners-Lee [2011]), URIs are specified in angular brackets and a triple may be specified by giving its subject, predicate and object followed by a period. Here is an example of two triples from DBpedia, expressing that Pelé played for the Brasilian soccer club Santos FC:

```
5. <http://dbpedia.org/resource/Pelé>
   <http://dbpedia.org/ontology/team>
   <http://dbpedia.org/resource/Santos_FC> .
```

Turtle has been a W3C recommended format since February 2013 and is used extensively in this book, as it is the most human-friendly representation of RDF.

In order to allow RDF documents to be represented even more tersely, it is possible to define prefixes to abbreviate URIs, by means of a `@prefix` declaration. Thus the previous example may be represented as follows:

```
6. @prefix dbpedia:  <http://dbpedia.org/ontology/> .
   @prefix resource: <http://dbpedia.org/resource/> .

   resource:Pelé dbpedia:team resource:Santos_FC .
```

String literals are specified with double quotes and may be followed by either an @ sign and a language tag, or by `^^` and a URI giving the data type of the literal. For example, the following two triples express that Pelé's full name is *Edison Arantes do Nascimento* and that he was born on October 23, 1940.

```
7. @prefix dbpedia:  <http://dbpedia.org/ontology/> .
   @prefix resource: <http://dbpedia.org/resource/> .
   @prefix dbpprop:  <http://dbpedia.org/property/> .
   @prefix xsd:      <http://www.w3.org/2001/XMLSchema#> .

   resource:Pelé dbpedia:fullname  "Edison Arantes do Nascimento"@en .
   resource:Pelé dbpedia:birthDate "1940-10-23"^^xsd:date .
```

Multiple triples with the same subject or same subject and predicate may be abbreviated by using semicolon and comma, which are considered to repeat the subject or subject and predicate respectively:

```
8. @prefix dbpedia:  <http://dbpedia.org/ontology/> .
   @prefix resource: <http://dbpedia.org/resource/> .

   resource:Pelé dbpedia:fullname "Edison Arantes do Nascimento"@en ;
           dbpedia:team resource:Santos_FC ,
                        resource:Bauru_Atlético_Clube ,
                        resource:Brazil_national_football_team .
```

In addition, the URI for an RDF type statement may be replaced by a, so the following two triples are equivalent:

```
9. resource:Pelé rdf:type dbpedia:SoccerPlayer .
   resource:Pelé a        dbpedia:SoccerPlayer .
```

Blank nodes in RDF correspond roughly to existentially quantified variables in first-order logic, and can be specified either by means of a blank node identifier prefixed by `_:`, or by means of square brackets. In the latter case extra triples may be stated within the brackets by specifying a predicate and an object (the subject is assumed to be the blank node). For example, the following two listings are equivalent:

```
10. resource:Pelé dbpedia:careerStation _:bn .
        _:bn    dbpedia:numberOfGoals "589" .

    resource:Pelé dbpedia:careerStation [ dbpedia:numberOfGoals "589" ].
```

It is generally not recommended to use blank nodes in RDF as they do not represent stable identifiers that can be referred to from other RDF datasets. Thus, the representation used in DBpedia for the listing above introduces an identifier for the career station:

```
11. resource:Pelé    dbpedia:careerStation resource:Pelé__2 .
    resource:Pelé__2 dbpedia:numberOfGoals "589" .
```

For more detailed introductions to RDF and Turtle, please consult the available W3C primers:

- http://www.w3.org/TR/rdf-primer/

- http://www.w3.org/2007/02/turtle/primer/

1.5   WHAT YOU NEED TO KNOW ABOUT SOCCER

People have enjoyed kicking a ball as a game for a long time, before the first set of common rules was carved out in 19th-century England. Love for the game spread over the world, and especially in Europe and the Americas you can find a lot of people for whom soccer is more than just a game. The popularity of soccer differs widely among the world's countries, and this also shows in the degree of professionalism. While the highest earning star players in Europe earn a yearly salary of over 20 million Euros, players in Bhutan or San Marino earn their living with regular day jobs, although their passion for the sport is often unmatched.

A soccer match is played by two teams with 11 players each—one *goalkeeper* and 10 field players. In addition, a referee (in official matches supported by several assistants) is responsible for keeping order and enforcing the rules.

The goal of the game is to get the ball into the opponent's goal, kicking it with the feet or the head, but not intentionally using the hands or generally any part of the arm, except for the goalkeeper, who is allowed to use his hands inside the penalty area in order to prevent the opponent from scoring. Field players usually play on fixed positions: the *defenders*' primary duty is to prevent the opponent from scoring, while the *midfielders*' main responsibility is to deliver balls from the defense forward to the *strikers*, whose main job is to score goals. The particular role of the players depends on the team's strategy and tactics, and it is common for defenders to go forward and even score, or for strikers to support the defense.

A match lasts 90 minutes and is divided into two halves of 45 minutes each and a half-time break of 15 minutes. It starts with the kick off, where the ball is in the middle of the field and all players in their own half, and ends with the referee's final whistle. The team that has scored the most goals wins.

Soccer is a physically demanding but not a brutal sport. Players are not allowed to hold, push or pull opponents, or to kick other things than the ball. If someone violates the rules, i.e., commits a *foul*, this is punished. Usually the other team is awarded a *free kick*, meaning that it will resume play from the spot of the foul, with the opponent having to keep some distance. If the foul was committed inside the other team's penalty area, this is considered particularly unfair as it might have prevented a clear scoring chance. In this case the fouled team is awarded a *penalty kick*, meaning that one player may take a free shot at the goal from the penalty spot, which is 12 yards (approximately 11 meters) away from the goal, defended only by the goalkeeper standing on the goal line. Depending on the foul, the player can also be punished with a *yellow card*, indicating a warning. Severe or repeated fouls are punished with a *red card*, dismissing the player from the game, of course without replacement.

The arguably most important and most celebrated soccer competition is the FIFA World Cup, taking place every four years since 1930 (except for 1942 and 1946, due to the Second World War). It is, in fact, one of the world's most widely viewed sports events. After a qualification round, the best teams compete for the title of world champion. The first World Cup winner was Uruguay, defeating Argentina in the finals. The team that has won the most World Cups so far is Brazil, which is also the only team that participated in every World Cup. After a group stage, all matches are knockout matches, which means that they need a winner. Therefore, if there is a draw after 90 minutes, there are 30 minutes of extra time. If this still does not yield a decision, the match

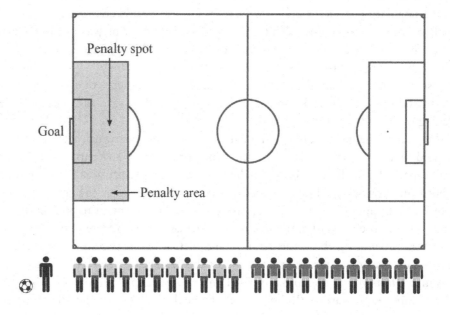

Figure 1.2: All you need for soccer: a field, two teams with 11 players each, a ball and a referee.

is decided by penalty shootouts. Penalty shootouts are often very dramatic, as they show that penalty kicks are not only about physical skills but also about the strength of the players' nerves.

Last but not least, an important part of every soccer match is the fans, not for nothing called *the 12th man*. Fan culture is an object of study on its own. The most visible and controverse fan movement is that of the *ultras* (ultra-fanatical supporters), easily recognizable by their banners and flags, and most known for their impressive choreography and singing as well as occasional outbursts of violence.

The examples in this book mention several of the greatest soccer players of all time. It is not necessary to know them in order to understand the examples, but we will briefly introduce them in order to give you some context:

- Pelé (Brazil) grew up in poverty but quickly rose to the *King of Football*. He is generally regarded as the greatest soccer player of all time.

- Ferenc Puskás (Hungary) was a brilliant goalgetter at the core of the legendary Hungarian team during the 1950s.

- Gerd Müller (Germany) was one of the most successful goalscorers ever.

- Eric Cantona (France), legend of Manchester United, was one of the most fascinating personalities in soccer—gifted, arrogant and sometimes violent, and besides a soccer player also an artist.

- George Best (Ireland) was an outstanding soccer player and soon became a celebrity, however not finding the right balance between his career and his extravagant lifestyle, finally succumbing to alcoholism.

- Johan Cruyff (The Netherlands), voted *European Player of the Century*, was best known for his precision and flexibility, being able to take over the position of any other player of the team.

- Diego Maradona (Argentina) was joint *FIFA Player of the 20th Century* with Pelé. Less laudably he coined the phrase *Hand of God* after scoring a World Cup goal by means of an unpenalized handball.

- Didier Drogba (Ivory Coast) is not only one of the best African soccer players but also known for his charity work and his help in bringing an end to the civil war in his country.

- Jan Koller (Czech Republic) was the leading goal scorer of his country, with an impressive physical presence due to his height of 2.02 m.

- Gianluigi Buffon (Italy) ranks among the best goalkeepers of the world.

- Lionel Messi (Argentina) is the top-scorer of Barcelona and widely recognized as the best living soccer player, an honor he is sharing with Cristiano Ronaldo (Portugal). He is not seldom compared with Pelé.

Of course this does not cover all there is to know about soccer, neither with respect to history and the rules nor with respect to the culture surrounding it. If you are looking for deeper insights into soccer, we recommend Galeano [2003].

CHAPTER 2

Ontologies

As we have seen in the introduction, ontologies play a central role in our approach to natural language interpretation, as they constitute the conceptual basis of the domain with respect to which natural language expressions will be interpreted. This chapter first introduces ontologies formally and then provides an example formalization for soccer domain knowledge using first-order logic and different flavors of description logics, in particular $\mathcal{ALC}$, OWL DL and OWL 2 DL. For this chapter we assume some background in logics as well as model-theoretic semantics.

2.1 DEFINING ONTOLOGIES

While there is no agreed-upon definition of ontologies, there are a number of popular definitions in computer science that are regularly cited by the community:[1]

- *an explicit specification of a conceptualization* [Gruber, 1993]

- *an explicit account or representation of [some part of] a conceptualization* [Uschold, 1996]

- *a logical theory accounting for the* intended meaning *of a formal vocabulary, i.e., its* ontological commitment *to a particular conceptualization of the world* [Guarino, 1998]

- *a formal explicit description of concepts in a domain of discourse* [Noy and McGuiness, 2001]

- *a formal, explicit specification of a shared conceptualization* [Studer et al., 1998]

Common to most of these definitions is the term *conceptualization*, which *is a world view*, i.e., it *corresponds to a way of thinking about some domain* [Uschold, 1996], and can be seen as *a set of informal rules that constrain the structure of a piece of reality* [Guarino, 1997]. Another common aspect of the definitions given above is that this conceptualization needs to be *explicit*. Further, some of the definitions require an ontology to be *formal* in the sense that it should have a formal semantics and be machine-readable as well as interpretable. Finally, some researchers require an ontology to be *shared* among different people.

The only formal definition of an ontology known to us is that of Guarino (see Guarino [1998] but also Guarino and Welty [2004]). We will recall the formal definition of an ontology below, but in essence an ontology according to Guarino is a logical theory that introduces a vocabulary and, by adding appropriate axioms, rules out unintended interpretations of this vocabulary

---

[1]Other possible interpretations of the term *ontology* can be found in Guarino and Giaretta [1995].

such that the models of the logical theory correspond to worlds, configurations or states of affairs that are possible with respect to the given conceptualization. An ontology in this sense defines what is not possible, i.e., which interpretations are not valid with respect to the way we intuitively understand these symbols.

Our goal when defining ontologies thus is that a system *understands* and *interprets* these symbols and draws appropriate inferences that are in line with our own understanding of the real-word counterparts that the symbols represent.

Before introducing a formal definition, let us look at an example. In the domain of soccer, there are (among other things) soccer players, soccer teams and soccer matches. We can introduce symbols representing these real-world sets of entities: `Player`, `Team` and `Match`. These are all unary logical predicates as they make assertions about which individuals belong to these sets or classes. Also of interest are relations between individuals, we therefore introduce a logical symbol `playsFor` representing the fact that a certain player plays for a team. This is thus a binary predicate relating a `Player` to a `Team`. Similarly, we can introduce binary predicates for representing the fact that a certain team participates in a match, `team`, or that a player plays in a certain match, `playsIn`.

For a machine, `Player`, `Team`, `playsFor`, etc. are just arbitrary symbols. However, as humans, we know that an individual that is a player cannot be a team or a match as well. We also know that there are exactly two teams participating in a match, that a player cannot play in two different matches at the same time, and that somebody who plays in a match for a team has to be a player. We know this because we have an understanding of the meaning and behavior of players, teams and matches in the real world. A computer lacks such an understanding and will have no trouble in assuming that some entity can be both a team and a match, that a match is member of a team, that a player can play in many different matches at the same time, and the like. As a result, a computer program might manipulate these symbols and perform inferences that do not correspond to our intuitive understanding of how the real-world counterparts of these symbols behave.

An ontology thus introduces semantic constraints to ensure that any instantiation of the vocabulary is in line with our understanding of the real-world counterparts that the single vocabulary elements denote. We can use different logical languages to express such constraints on how the symbols are to be used. Using first-order logic, some of the above constraints could be formalized as follows.

- The set of matches and players are disjoint:
  $\forall x\, (\texttt{Match}(x) \rightarrow \neg\texttt{Player}(x))$

- A player can play only in one match at a time:
  $\forall p, m_1, m_2\, (\texttt{playsIn}(p, m_1) \wedge \texttt{playsIn}(p, m_2) \wedge \texttt{temporalOverlap}(m_1, m_2)$
  $\rightarrow m_1 = m_2)$

- It is players that play for teams:
  $\forall x, y \ (\mathtt{playsFor}(x, y) \rightarrow \mathtt{Player}(x) \land \mathtt{Team}(y))$

Given these examples, we are now ready to introduce the formal definition of ontologies according to Guarino, specifying what it exactly means that an ontology is a *formal specification of a conceptualization*. Before introducing this definition, we will define the notions of a *world*, a *domain space* and a *conceptual relation*. In all the definitions we assume that our scope is a certain system S which can be fully described by a set of variables and their possible values. A *world* then represents a possible configuration in which the system can be, thus being a *maximal observable state of affairs*, i.e., an assignment of values to all observable values that characterize a system.

Definition 2.1 Domain space   Given a system S, we call a pair $\langle D, W \rangle$ a *domain space*, where D is a set of distinguished elements and W is a set of worlds (see above).

Definition 2.2 Conceptual relation   Given a certain system S as well as a corresponding domain space (D, W), we call a function $\rho^n \colon W \rightarrow \mathcal{P}(D^n)$ a *conceptual relation*, where $\mathcal{P}(D^n)$ denotes the power set of all n-tuples over D. We say that ρ has arity n.

A conceptual relation ρ thus represents the extension of a certain relation between elements of D in a given world w. In our example, Player would be a conceptual relation of arity 1 with $\rho(w) \subseteq D$ and represents the set of all soccer players who exist in world w.

We are now ready to define what a *conceptualization* is.

Definition 2.3 Conceptualization   A conceptualization $\mathcal{C}$ is a triple $(D, W, \mathcal{R})$ with

- D a universe of discourse,

- W a set of possible worlds,

- $\mathcal{R}$ a set of conceptual relations over (D, W).

Such a conceptualization is typically *implicit* in the mind of an agent that perceives and acts in the world. However, for a computer system to be able to perform inferences that are in line with a given conceptualization, i.e., a way of understanding the world, this conceptualization needs to be made explicit. There is a practical and an impractical variant of making such a conceptualization explicit. The impractical one consists in specifying the extension of the conceptual relations for each world. This might be impossible as the number of worlds can be infinite. The practical one consists in specifying the possible extensions in different worlds intensionally, e.g., by an appropriate logical theory. It is the latter type of specification that we are interested in, i.e., designing a logical theory (an ontology) the models of which correspond as closely as possible to the different worlds that are possible according to the conceptualization.

The question is how we capture the relation between a logical theory that constrain the behavior of the symbols in our vocabulary and a given conceptualization of the world. This correspondence is called *ontological commitment* of a logical vocabulary, i.e., what the symbols *mean* with respect to a given conceptualization.

Definition 2.4 Ontological commitment Let T be a logical theory with vocabulary V expressed in some logical language. An *ontological commitment* for this theory T is a pair $(C, \mathcal{I})$, where $C = (D, W, \mathcal{R})$ is a conceptualization and $\mathcal{I}$ is a function $\mathcal{I} \colon V \to D \cup \mathcal{R}$.

Thus, an ontological commitment defines how the symbols used in a given logical theory are to be interpreted with respect to the conceptualization.

Guarino now defines *intended models* of the logical theory. Intuitively, intended models are those that represent a state of affairs that corresponds to some possible world according to the conceptualization. A model $M = ((D, \mathcal{R}), I)$ in our sense consists of a domain $(D, \mathcal{R})$ that fixes a set D of individuals as well as the logical vocabulary by defining a set $\mathcal{R}$ of conceptual relations. I is then the standard interpretation function that assigns extensions with respect to D to all vocabulary elements.

Definition 2.5 Intended model Let $C = (D, W, \mathcal{R})$ be a conceptualization and T a logical theory with vocabulary V expressed in some logical language. Further, let $\mathcal{K}$ be an ontological commitment $\mathcal{K} = (C, \mathcal{I})$. A model $M = ((D, \mathcal{R}), I)$ of T is called an *intended model* according to $\mathcal{K}$ if and only if

- for all constants c in V: $I(c) = \mathcal{I}(c)$, and

- there is a world w such that for all predicates p in V: $I(p) = (\mathcal{I}(p))(w)$.

That is, for constants the interpretation function I of the model and the ontological commitment $\mathcal{I}$ map that constant to the same element in D. For predicates p there needs to be some world w such that the extension of the relation ρ that represents the ontological commitment of p in world w is the same as the extension assigned to p by the interpretation function I of the model. The set $I_{\mathcal{K}}(T)$ represents the set of all intended models of the theory T according to $\mathcal{K}$.

Intuitively, our goal is to design the logical theory in such a way that every model of the logical theory corresponds to at least one possible world and each possible world corresponds to at least one model. This is formalized as follows:

Definition 2.6 Ontology Given a conceptualization C, an ontology O is a logical theory with an ontological commitment $\mathcal{K}$ such that the models of the logical theory *approximate as well as possible the set of intended models* $I_{\mathcal{K}}(O)$ (see Oberle et al. [2009]).

Hereby, a logical theory approximates perfectly the set of intended models if every intended model corresponds to a valid world state according to the conceptualization and every world state corresponds to one or more models. Note that the granularity of the vocabulary used in the ontology can differ from the conceptual relations available in the conceptualization so that a one-to-one mapping between models will not hold in the general case. In case the ontological vocabulary is less fine-grained, several world states will be conflated in one model of the ontology.

If the ontology has models that are non-intended according to the conceptualization, the ontology is *overgenerating* as it might miss important inferences and in this sense would be incomplete with respect to the conceptualization. This is in particular the case if certain constraints cannot be expressed given the logical language in question. Consider the example of conceptualizing *men* and *women*. Assume that a conceptualization specifies two conceptual relations Man and Woman of arity 1. And suppose that there is no possible world according to the conceptualization in which they share elements, i.e., $\forall w \in W$ (Man$(w) \cap$ Woman$(w) = \emptyset$). Now assume a logical language that cannot express disjointness between sets. In such a language, it would be impossible to rule out models in which the extension of the predicates that commit to the relations Man and Woman share elements. So, given a certain logical language, there are limits to how good the alignment between models and possible worlds is. This, however, is acceptable in principle as it will not generate wrong inferences.

According to Guarino, the critical situation is the one in which the ontology *undergenerates*, i.e., rules out intended models. This situation is critical because the ontological theory may become *unsound* in the sense of producing inferences that are not valid in all worlds. The different configurations are illustrated in Figure 2.1 [Oberle et al., 2009].

2.2   ONTOLOGIES IN FIRST-ORDER LOGIC

We briefly discuss how first-order logic can be used to formulate ontological knowledge, using examples from the domain of soccer. The vocabulary we will consider is the following:

- *Unary predicates:* Match, Goal, SoccerAction, GoalDirectedAction, PlayerDirectedAction, Freekick, Cornerkick, Foul

- *Binary predicates:* winner, loser, byPlayer, forTeam, inMatch, playsIn, happensAt

- *Ternary predicates:* playsFor

- *Functions:* score (taking three arguments, a team, a match and a time point, and returning an integer representing the number of goals achieved by the team until this time point), end (taking one argument, a time interval, and returning a time point at which the match began), begins (taking one argument, a time interval, and returning a time point at which the match ended)

From now on, we follow the typical convention in the Semantic Web community of writing unary predicates or class predicates with initial upper case letters, while relations and properties

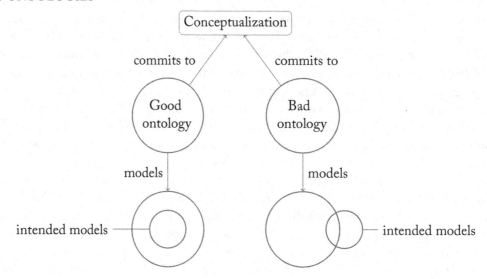

Figure 2.1: Relation between conceptualization, models and intended models: good and bad ontologies according to Guarino.

are written with initial lower case letters. Using the above vocabulary, we can axiomatize some basic knowledge about the soccer domain as follows:

- A freekick is a goal-directed action.

$$\forall x \ (\texttt{Freekick}(x) \rightarrow \texttt{GoalDirectedAction}(x))$$

- A foul is a player-directed action.

$$\forall x \ (\texttt{Foul}(x) \rightarrow \texttt{PlayerDirectedAction}(x))$$

- A goal is always accomplished in a certain match m, by a certain player p and for a certain team t, and it happens at a certain time interval i.

$$\forall g \ (\texttt{Goal}(g) \rightarrow \exists t, m, p, i \ (\texttt{inMatch}(g, m) \wedge \texttt{forTeam}(g, t) \wedge \\ \texttt{byPlayer}(g, p) \wedge \texttt{happensAt}(g, i)))$$

- There are exactly two teams per match.

$$\forall m \ (\texttt{Match}(m) \rightarrow \exists t_1, t_2 \ (\texttt{team}(m, t_1) \wedge \texttt{team}(m, t_2) \wedge t_1 \neq t_2 \wedge \\ \forall t \ (\texttt{team}(m, t) \rightarrow t = t_1 \vee t = t_2)))$$

- If one team wins the match, then the other team loses it.

$$\forall m, w, l \; ((\text{Match}(m) \wedge \text{team}(m, w) \wedge \text{team}(m, l) \wedge w \neq l \wedge$$
$$\text{winner}(m, w)) \rightarrow \text{loser}(m, l))$$

- If a soccer player plays in a soccer match, he cannot play in another match at the same time.[2]

$$\forall m_1, m_2, p, t_1, t_2 \; (\text{Match}(m_1) \wedge \text{Match}(m_2) \wedge$$
$$\text{playsIn}(p, m_1) \wedge \text{matchDuration}(m_1, t_1) \wedge$$
$$\text{playsIn}(p, m_2) \wedge \text{matchDuration}(m_2, t_2) \wedge$$
$$\text{overlap}(t_1, t_2) \rightarrow m_1 = m_2)$$

- If the score of a team is higher than the score of the other team at the end of the game, then the former is the winner.[3]

$$\forall m, t_1, t_2, t \; ((\text{Match}(m) \wedge \text{team}(m, t_1) \wedge \text{team}(m, t_2) \wedge$$
$$\text{matchDuration}(m, t) \wedge$$
$$\text{score}(t_1, m, \text{end}(t)) > \text{score}(t_2, m, \text{end}(t)))$$
$$\rightarrow \text{winner}(m, t_1))$$

These axioms are good examples of how first-order logic can be used to define an ontology.

Exercise 2.7   Write down a small ontology in first-order logic that axiomatizes family relationships, in particular father, mother, son, daughter, uncle, aunt, grandfather, and grandmother.

Exercise 2.8   Does your ontology from Exercise 2.7 have unintended models? Is it possible that someone is his or her own father or mother or his or her own son or daughter? If yes, then correct your ontology appropriately by ruling out these unintended interpretations.

We now turn to description logics as a family of languages similar to first-order logic that form the backbone of current ontology formalisms in the context of the Semantic Web, in particular the *Web Ontology Language* (OWL).

---

[2]Where overlap can be defined using predicates from Chapter 8 as follows: $\forall t_1, t_2 \; (\text{overlap}(t_1, t_2) \equiv \text{intOverlap}(t_1, t_2) \vee \text{intOverlap}(t_2, t_1) \vee \text{intEqual}(t_1, t_2) \vee \text{intStarts}(t_1, t_2) \vee \text{intFinishes}(t_1, t_2) \vee \text{intStarts}(t_2, t_1) \vee \text{intFinishes}(t_2, t_1)).$

[3]Here we assume the availability of a predicate $>$ either in the model-theoretic semantics or as built-in operator in a reasoner.

2.3   ONTOLOGIES IN DESCRIPTION LOGICS

The drawback of first-order logic for representing ontological knowledge is that it is undecidable. For this reason, over the last decades researchers have introduced decidable fragments of first-order logic as a basis for capturing ontological knowledge. A popular family of fragments of first-order logic are so-called *description logic languages*. They have also been called *terminological logics* as their main application has been to axiomatize terms, or concepts, as well as (subsumption) relations between them.

A very simple yet popular description logic language that we will consider for illustration purposes is $\mathcal{ALC}$, first introduced by Schmidt-Schauß and Smolka [1991]. It is the smallest description logic that is closed under Boolean operations. The basis of $\mathcal{ALC}$ are so-called *class expressions* of the form below. From now on A will refer to an atomic concept, while C and D will refer to complex concepts. R stands for a binary relation or binary predicate, which in description logics are called *roles*.

$$C, D := A \mid \top \mid \bot \mid \neg C \mid C \sqcap D \mid C \sqcup D \mid \forall R.C \mid \exists R.C$$

In what follows we give a short, intuitive explanation of the meaning of these class expressions:

- $\top$ is the set of all things (typically called *top*)

- $\bot$ is the empty set (typically called *bottom*)

- $\neg C$ is the set of all things that are not members of class C

- $C \sqcap D$ is the set of all things that are members of classes C and D

- $C \sqcup D$ is the set of all things that are members of class C or members of class D

- $\forall R.C$ is the set of all things that are related through R only to members of class C

- $\exists R.C$ is the set of all things that are related to at least one member of class C through relation R

The most important statements in a description logic language are so-called *general class inclusion axioms* (GCIs) stating that two concepts are related by subsumption. GCIs have the form $C \sqsubseteq D$ and are equivalent to the first-order logic statement $\forall x\ (C(x) \rightarrow D(x))$.

Given this very informal characterization of description logics using $\mathcal{ALC}$ as an example, let us now look at which axioms of our soccer ontology we can capture in $\mathcal{ALC}$.

- A freekick is a goal-directed action.

$$\text{Freekick} \sqsubseteq \text{GoalDirectedAction}$$

- A foul is a player-directed action.

$$\text{Foul} \sqsubseteq \text{PlayerDirectedAction}$$

- A goal is always accomplished by a certain player and for a certain team.

$$\text{Goal} \sqsubseteq \exists\,\texttt{inMatch.Match} \sqcap \exists\,\texttt{forTeam.Team} \sqcap \exists\,\texttt{byPlayer.Player} \sqcap$$
$$\exists\,\texttt{happensAt.Instant}$$

Actually, this axiom is more restrictive than the corresponding first-order logic axiom discussed above as it also restricts the types of things standing in the `inMatch`, `forTeam`, `byPlayer` and `happensffAt` relations to `Match`, `Team`, `Player` and `Instant`, respectively.

- That there are exactly two teams per match cannot be directly expressed in $\mathcal{ALC}$, but we will see that this is possible in other description logics which can express so-called *number restrictions*.

- The axiom expressing that a team loses a match if the other one wins it requires establishing an implication of one relation (`loser`) by another one (`winner`), which cannot be expressed in $\mathcal{ALC}$.

- The axiom that a player cannot play in more than one match at the same time is not expressible in $\mathcal{ALC}$ as it requires five universally quantified variables as well as so-called property chains that are only available in more expressive description logics.

- The axiom expressing the fact that a team wins a match if the score of that team is higher than the score of the other team at the end of the game involves four universally quantified variables as well as an implicational property chain that cannot be expressed in $\mathcal{ALC}$.

So we have seen that there are some axioms (though not all of them) of our toy soccer ontology that can be expressed in the simple description logic $\mathcal{ALC}$. Let us now turn to more expressive description logics and see what they can do. Description logics are named using acronyms according to the following scheme:

- $\mathcal{S}$ stands for $\mathcal{ALC}$ plus *role transitivity*, allowing us to express transitivity of some relation R:
$$Trans(R) \equiv \forall x, y, z \ (R(x, y) \wedge R(y, z) \rightarrow R(x, z))$$

- $\mathcal{H}$ stands for *role hierarchies*, allowing us to express inclusion axioms between *roles*, in the simplest case saying that some role R subsumes some other role R':
$$R' \sqsubseteq R \equiv \forall x, y \ (R'(x, y) \rightarrow R(x, y))$$

- $\mathcal{O}$ stands for *nominals*. These are classes that consist of exactly one individual a. We will write such nominals as $\{a\}$.

- $\mathcal{I}$ stands for *inverse roles*. We can say that a role R^- is the inverse of a role R:
$$\forall x, y \ (R(x, y) \rightarrow R^-(y, x))$$

- $\mathcal{N}$ stands for *cardinality restrictions* that allow us to express that there is a maximum or minimum number of individuals n to which some element can be related to via a given relation R. We write $\leq_n R$ to represent the set of all x for which $|\{y \mid R(x, y)\}| \leq n$. Analogously, we write $\geq_n R$ for the set of all x for which $|\{y \mid R(x, y)\}| \geq n$, and $=_n R$ for the set of all x for which $|\{y \mid R(x, y)\}| = n$.

- $\mathcal{D}$ stands for *datatypes* including strings, numbers, dates, etc.

- $\mathcal{F}$ stands for *role functionality*:

$$Func(R) \equiv \forall x, y, z \ (R(x, y) \wedge R(x, z) \rightarrow y = z)$$

Note that cardinality restrictions subsume role functionality as we can say $\top \sqsubseteq \leq_1 R$.

- $\mathcal{Q}$ stands for *qualified cardinality restrictions*, which allow us to express that there are at most n individuals of class C that a certain individual x can be related to through role R. We write $\leq nR.C$ for the set of all x for which $|\{y \mid R(x, y) \wedge C(y)\}| \leq n$ and analogously $\geq_n R.C$ and $=_n R.C$. Qualified cardinality restrictions obviously subsume unqualified cardinality restrictions.

- $\mathcal{R}$ stands for *generalized role inclusion axioms* and other features. The general form of a generalized role inclusion axiom looks as follows:

$$R_1 \circ R_2 \circ \ldots \circ R_{n-1} \sqsubseteq R_n \equiv$$
$$\forall x_1, x_2, \ldots, x_n \ R_1(x_1, x_2) \wedge R_2(x_2, x_3) \cdots R_{n-1}(x_{n-1}, x_n) \rightarrow R(x_1, x_n)$$

This obviously subsumes role hierarchies.

- $\mathcal{E}$ stands for the use of *existential role restrictions*.

Now we will consider two members of the family of description logic languages that correspond to OWL DL ($\mathcal{SHOIN}(\mathbf{D})$) and OWL 2 DL ($\mathcal{SROIQ}$), respectively. We will then discuss to what extent our soccer ontology can be axiomatized in these logics.

2.3.1   OWL DL OR $\mathcal{SHOIN}(\mathbf{D})$

OWL DL corresponds to the language $\mathcal{SHOIN}(\mathbf{D})$, which includes the following: $\mathcal{S}$ ($\mathcal{ALC}$ plus role transitivity), $\mathcal{H}$ (role hierarchies), $\mathcal{O}$ (nominals), $\mathcal{I}$ (inverse roles), $\mathcal{N}$ (cardinality restrictions), and $\mathcal{D}$ (datatypes). Let us look at which of our axioms that could not be expressed in $\mathcal{ALC}$ can now be expressed in $\mathcal{SHOIN}(\mathbf{D})$:

- There are exactly two teams per match. This can be expressed by a cardinality restriction on relation `team`, specifying that for each match there are exactly two teams:

$$\text{Match} \sqsubseteq =_2 \text{team}$$

- If one team wins the match, then the other team loses it. As already mentioned above, we need so-called generalized role inclusion axioms for this, which are not available in OWL DL, but in OWL 2 DL (see Section 2.3.2 below).

- If a soccer player plays in a soccer match, he cannot play in another match at the same time. As above, this cannot be expressed because role inclusion axioms are needed.

- If the score of a team is higher than the score of the other team at the end of the game, then the former is the winner. Here we have the same problem as with the preceding axiom.

Exercise 2.9 Download some ontology editor, for instance Protégé, which you can find at `http://protege.stanford.edu/`.

- Install and start it.

- Add the following soccer-related classes: `Match`, `SoccerAction`, `PlayerDirectedAction`, `GoalDirectedAction`, `Score`, `Team`, `Goal`. Model the hierarchical (subsumption) relations between these classes.

- Add subclasses of `PlayerDirectedAction` (e.g., `Foul`) as well as subclasses of `GoalDirectedAction` (e.g., `PenaltyKick`).

- Model the disjointness relations between these classes.

- Model the fact that all soccer events (i.e., goals and actions, whether player or goal directed) have a certain minute at which they occur. Also model the fact that a goal is always achieved by a certain player and for a certain team.

- Model that a score holds in a certain match, for a certain team and at a certain minute of the match.

- Add an axiom that states that there are exactly two (different) teams playing in a match.

2.3.2 OWL 2 DL OR $\mathcal{SROIQ}(\mathbf{D})$

The ontology language OWL 2 DL[4] corresponds to the description logic $\mathcal{SROIQ}(\mathbf{D})$, which includes $\mathcal{S}$ ($\mathcal{ALC}$ plus role transitivity), $\mathcal{H}$ (role hierarchies), $\mathcal{O}$ (nominals), $\mathcal{I}$ (inverse roles), $\mathcal{N}$ (cardinality restrictions), $\mathbf{D}$ (datatypes), $\mathcal{Q}$ (qualified cardinality restrictions, thus subsuming $\mathcal{N}$), and $\mathcal{R}$ (generalized role inclusion axioms, thus subsuming role hierarchies).

Before discussing to what extent our soccer axioms can be represented in $\mathcal{SROIQ}(\mathbf{D})$, we will have a more detailed look at the types of classes that can be expressed and which role

---

[4]`http://www.w3.org/TR/owl2-direct-semantics/`

inclusion axioms are allowed. Assuming that C and D are classes, a is an individual, R is a simple role[5] and S is an arbitrary role, the admitted class expressions are the following ones:

$$\neg C \mid C \sqcap D \mid C \sqcup D \mid \{a\} \mid \forall R.C \mid \exists R.C \mid \exists S.Self \mid \leq_n S.C \mid \geq_n S.C$$

We have discussed most of these class constructs already above, with the exception of $\exists S.Self$ which refers to the class of things that are related to themselves via the role S, i.e., $\exists r.Self \equiv \{x \mid r(x, x)\}$.

Generalized role inclusion axioms can take one of the following forms:

- *Transitivity:* $R \circ R \sqsubseteq R$

- *Symmetry:* $R^- \sqsubseteq R$

- $S_1 \circ \ldots \circ S_n \sqsubseteq R$

- $R \circ S_1 \circ \ldots \circ \sqsubseteq R$

- $S_1 \circ \ldots \circ S_n \circ R \sqsubseteq R$

A set of axioms of these forms is called a generalized role hierarchy.

For all the mentioned generalized role inclusion axioms it must hold that $S_i \prec R$ for all numbers i, where $\prec$ is a total order[6] between roles. This requirement is necessary to avoid recursion and thus cyclic generalized role hierarchies leading to undecidability. However, OWL 2 DL allows for some limited recursion, allowing the use of roles at the right-hand side of the implication as first or last element in a chain.

Additionally, OWL 2 DL allows for expressing disjointness, asymmetry and reflexivity of roles:

- *Disjointness:* $Disjoint(R_1, R_2) \equiv \forall x, y R_1(x, y) \rightarrow \neq R_2(x, y)$

- *Asymmetry:* $Asy(R) \equiv \forall x, y R(x, y) \rightarrow \neq R(y, x)$

- *Reflexivity:* $Ref(R) \equiv \forall x R(x, x)$

Generalized role inclusion are in essence very similar to Horn rules, which are a special subset of first-order implications of the following form:

$$\forall x_1, x_2, \cdots, x_n \ p_1(x_1, \ldots, x_n) \wedge \cdots \wedge p_m(x_1, \ldots, x_n) \rightarrow p(x_1, \ldots, x_n)$$

This brings up the question which subset of Horn rules can be expressed in $\mathcal{SROIQ}(\mathbf{D})$. First of all, for a Horn rule to be expressible in OWL 2 DL, all predicates p_i need to be binary.

---

[5] A simple role is a role that does not occur on the right-hand side of a role inclusion axiom and neither does the inverse of this role. For an inductive and complete definition of simple roles, see Hitzler et al. [2009, page 169].

[6] In mathematics, a total order is a binary relation (here denoted by infix $\prec$) on some set X. Such a relation is transitive, antisymmetric, and total in the sense that for $\forall \ x, y x \prec y \vee y \prec x$.

Given this, there is a simple algorithm to determine whether a Horn rule can be represented in $\mathcal{SROIQ}(\mathbf{D})$: We plot all variables occurring in the rule in a graph, adding an edge between variables if they appear in the same predicate in the premise, i.e., the left-hand side of the implication. A Horn rule is expressible in $\mathcal{SROIQ}(\mathbf{D})$ if and only if there is at most one undirected path between any two variables in the premises (see Hitzler et al. [2009, pages 226–229] for technical details).

Additionally, there are two specific constructs that sometimes are required when writing role inclusion axioms. One is the universal role U defined as $\{(x, x) \mid \top(x)\}$, and the other one is the class $R_C.Self$ defining a relation R_C through which all members of the class C are related to themselves, i.e., the class $\{(x, x) \mid C(x)\}$.

We will refer to Horn rules that can be expressed as OWL 2 DL generalized role inclusion axioms as *description logic rules*.

Now we can try to axiomatize the remaining axioms of our soccer ontology using OWL 2 DL:

- If one team wins a match, then the other team loses it. This can be expressed by the following Horn rule:

$$\forall m, w, l \; ((\texttt{Match}(m) \wedge \texttt{team}(m, w) \wedge \texttt{team}(m, l) \wedge w \neq l \wedge$$
$$\texttt{winner}(m, w) \rightarrow \texttt{loser}(m, l))$$

The following undirected graph connecting variables appearing in the same predicate shows that there are two paths between the variables m and w, i.e., one direct edge as well as the path through l:

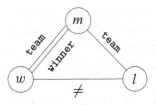

Hence, unfortunately, the rule cannot be expressed in OWL 2 DL as a generalized role inclusion axiom. However, the following set of axioms will do the same job:

$$\texttt{winner} \sqsubseteq \texttt{team}$$
$$\texttt{loser} \sqsubseteq \texttt{team}$$
$$\exists\,\texttt{winner}.\top \equiv \exists\,\texttt{loser}.\top$$
$$Disjoint(\texttt{winner}, \texttt{loser})$$
$$\texttt{Match} \sqsubseteq\, =_2 \texttt{team}$$

The above axioms express the fact that each x that is a winner/loser is also a team (first two axioms). Further, the third axiom states that the class of games with a winner is equivalent to the class of games with a loser, i.e., allowing us to derive that if there is a winner, then there is also a loser and the other way round. Further, winner and loser are disjoint, and each match has exactly two teams. As long as we state that there is a winner, it would follow with the third axiom that there is also a loser. The winner is one of the two teams of the match. It follows that the loser is the other of the two teams as there are exactly two of them and there has to be a winner which is disjoint to the loser.

- If a soccer player plays in a soccer match, he cannot play in another match at the same time. This can be expressed by the following Horn rule:

$$\forall p, g_1, g_2, t_1, t_2 \ (\text{Player}(p) \land \text{playsIn}(p, g_1) \land \text{matchDuration}(g_1, t_1) \land$$
$$\text{overlap}(t_1, t_2) \land \text{matchDuration}(g_2, t_2)$$
$$\rightarrow \neg\text{playsIn}(p, g_2))$$

As a first shot, we might transform this into the following rule chain axiom:

$$R_{\text{Player}} \circ \text{playsIn} \circ \text{matchDuration} \circ \text{overlap} \circ \text{matchDuration}^-$$
$$\sqsubseteq \text{notPlaysIn}$$

However, notPlaysIn is not a simple role here as it is defined in terms of other roles. As a consequence it cannot participate in any disjointness axioms, i.e., we would not be able to express that *Disjoint*(notPlaysIn, playsInGame).

- If the score of a team is higher than the score of the other team at the end of the game, then the former is the winner. We have represented this axiom in first-order logic using a function score with three arguments. Functions unfortunately cannot be represented in description logics. Moreover, all roles in description logics have two arguments. We would therefore need to reify a score, introducing a class Score together with four roles: inMatch, atMinute and forTeam corresponding to the three arguments, and value for the return value. We could then rewrite our axiom as follows:

$$\forall m, t_1, t_2, t \ ((\text{Match}(m) \land \text{team}(m, t_1) \land \text{team}(m, t_2) \land$$
$$\text{matchDuration}(m, t) \land \text{Score}(s_1) \land \text{Score}(s_2) \land$$
$$\text{atMinute}(s_1, 90) \land \text{forTeam}(s_1, t_1) \land \text{inMatch}(s_1, m) \land$$
$$\text{atMinute}(s_2, 90) \land \text{forTeam}(s_2, t_2) \land \text{inMatch}(s_2, m) \land$$
$$\text{value}(s_1, v_1) \land \text{value}(s_2, v_2) \land v_1 > v_2)$$
$$\rightarrow \text{winner}(m, t_1))$$

Unfortunately, this axiom cannot be translated into OWL 2 DL, as the following graph relating the variables in the premises shows:

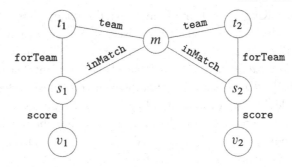

Exercise 2.10   Add a property chain to your ontology stating that a soccer player can only play in one game at a time.

Exercise 2.11   Formalize the conditions under which two intervals can be said to temporally overlap. Formalize this relation `overlap` in OWL 2 DL.

Exercise 2.12   The concept of an opener, as it occurred in the very first example sentence of this book, expresses that a goal is the first goal that happened in a match. Is it possible to formalize this concept in OWL 2 DL? Independent of the formalization, could it be inferred from a knowledge base that some goal is an opener? (Take into account that OWL relies on the open-world assumption.)

The goal of this chapter has been to formally introduce the notion of an ontology and to give an overview of well-known languages for modeling ontological knowledge. We have discussed first-order language and various flavors of description logics to formalize ontological knowledge. We have seen that languages vary in their expressiveness and thus in the world knowledge that they can model, also affecting how well an ontology approximates the given conceptualization. We have highlighted the limits of various languages on the basis of the case of modeling knowledge about the soccer domain as an illustrating example.

2.4   FURTHER READING

The soccer ontology can be downloaded at the book website.

The only formal approach to ontology engineering (in the sense of introducing formal conditions that can be verified) is due to Guarino, see Guarino [1998] and Guarino and Welty [2000], and has been implemented in the so-called OntoClean methodology [Guarino and Welty, 2004]. Many *ontology engineering methodologies* that define the important steps of the ontology engineering lifecycle have been proposed. Examples of early ontology engineering methodologies are the one by Uschold and King [1995], the Unified Methodology [Uschold, 1996] or METHON-TOLOGY [Fernández-Lopez et al., 1997]. Recent methodologies have stressed argumentative and collaborative aspects of ontology engineering (e.g., Tempich et al. [2007]; Tudorache et al. [2013]) and focused in particular on reuse, also of non-ontological resources (see Villazón-Terrazas et al. [2010]). A first guide to ontology engineering, using the case of developing a wine ontology as example, has been formulated by Noy and McGuiness [2001]. More details about description logics can be found in the description logics handbook [Baader et al., 2003]. A nice introductory textbook about the Semantic Web is the one by Hitzler et al. [2009], which also includes extensive discussion of the logical foundations of OWL DL and RDF. An overview of documentation of OWL and RDF can be found at `http://www.w3.org/TR/owl2-overview/` and `http://www.w3.org/RDF/`, respectively.

CHAPTER 3

Linguistic Formalisms

In natural language processing, the question of which linguistic formalism to choose is often answered on the basis of their adequacy for a particular task, or following practical considerations, such as the availability of software tools and language resources. In this chapter we present grammar formalisms that have proved useful and well-suited for the task of ontology-based interpretation of natural language. However, nothing essential hinges on using these particular formalisms and we would like to encourage you to try out the examples in this book in the grammar formalism of your choice.

We will start with a very brief introduction to what grammars are and what we mean when we talk about ontology-based grammars. Then we will present two particular formalisms for syntactic and semantic representations: *Lexicalized Tree Adjoining Grammars* (LTAG) and *Dependency-based Underspecified Discourse Representation Structures* (DUDES). Finally, we will show how such representations can be aligned to an ontology and then used for parsing and interpretation.

3.1 FORM AND MEANING

Grammars are explicit descriptions of the rules of a language, usually addressing different levels of granularity. We will not investigate the sounds of a language, how sounds build the basis for the smallest meaning-distinguishing and meaning-carrying units of a language, or how those units combine to form words. Rather, we are interested in those levels that concern the structure and the meaning of the expressions of a language:

- *Syntax* studies how words are combined into phrases and sentences.

- *Semantics* investigates the meanings of expressions of a language, and how the meanings of basic expressions are combined into meanings of more complex expressions.

Although we talk about words, we are agnostic with respect to the question of what exactly a word is. As a rough approximation, we can assume that a word is a unit that bears meaning and can be uttered in isolation. Of course, as soon as you think about synthetic languages, this gets more complicated. For the purposes of this book we will sidestep this discussion, although it is good to be aware of it.

There is a range of syntactic and semantic formalisms, and a number of possibilities of how to couple them into a theory of both form and meaning. A very popular view on grammar that we adopt in this book is the following: Syntax defines basic elements (strings, typed strings, trees, feature representations, etc.) and processes that combine these basic elements into more complex structures. Semantics specifies what meanings are and how they can be combined. Furthermore, every basic syntactic element is paired with a meaning (or several meanings in the case of ambiguities, see Chapter 7), and every syntactic rule that combines two elements is paired with corresponding semantic rules that combine their meanings. In this way, syntax and semantics are tightly connected: A grammar starts from atomic expressions comprising both a form and a meaning, and then constructs the form and meaning of more complex expressions compositionally.

There are a number of syntactic and semantic formalisms that can be exploited for instantiating this view on grammar. As already mentioned in the very beginning of the chapter, we choose two formalisms that are flexible with respect to their basic building blocks and therefore prove well-suited for our purposes; we will see this in the course of the chapter. But this, of course, does not mean that these formalisms are the only ones that are suitable for ontology-based interpretation. If you arrive at the end of the chapter with a clear understanding of what an ontology-based grammar is, you are invited to pick any grammar formalism you know and think about how you could align it to an ontology.

3.2   SYNTACTIC REPRESENTATIONS: LTAG

Tree Adjoining Grammar (TAG) [Joshi, 1985; Joshi et al., 1975] is a linguistic formalism that builds on trees as representations of syntactic structure, like many other grammar formalisms. But while other formalisms focus on strings and how to combine them into tree structures, TAG starts from trees as basic building blocks. That is, the atomic elements are structured objects already. The reason to start with structured objects as basic building blocks is to provide a large enough domain of locality, such that all syntactic dependencies and constraints such as agreement can be captured within one atomic (or: elementary) tree. This idea is at the very core of TAG.

TAG's fundamental hypothesis (Frank [2002]). *Every syntactic dependency is expressed locally within a single elementary tree.*

Since this would also be the case if elementary trees comprised whole sentences (a quite uninteresting case when you actually want to study processes of structure composition), Frank [2002] formulated a constraint that restricts the size of elementary trees, requiring that every elementary tree comprises the so-called *extended projection* of a single lexical head—nothing less and nothing more. This keeps elementary trees as minimal as possible, while at the same time allowing them to be as big as necessary for the above hypothesis to hold. The extended projection of a lexical item roughly contains all elements that directly depend on it, especially those that it subcategorizes for and thus provides the domain for many grammatical processes. The verb to like, for example, subcategorizes for two noun phrase elements: a subject (the one who likes) and an object (that which is liked). The extended projection of this verb thus contains both, and provides the scene for agreement processes, for example, like number agreement as in she likes and they like. For the

Category symbol	Full category name	Examples
S	sentence	Uruguay won every game.
V	verb	sleep, like, give
NP	noun phrase	game, team
DET	determiner	the, a, every, no
DP	determiner phrase	no game, John
ADJ	adjective	brave
ADV	adverb	bravely
P	preposition	of, into, with
PP	prepositional phrase	into the wild, with a smile
POSS	possessive ending	's
REL	relative pronoun	who, which, that

Figure 3.1: Syntactic categories.

exact definition of elementary tree minimality, see Frank [2002]. In Section 3.3 below, we will slightly extend elementary trees in order to align them to ontology concepts.

In addition to elementary trees, TAG provides operations for combining trees into larger tree structures. A tree adjoining grammar therefore consists of two basic ingredients: elementary trees (*initial* and *auxiliary trees*), and structure-building operations that expand and combine trees (*substitution* and *adjunction*). Let us look at both in more detail.

Trees are directed acyclic graphs. As common in syntactic formalisms, we take leaf nodes to be strings and assume that branching nodes are labeled with syntactic categories. The table in Figure 3.1 specifies the categories that we are going to use throughout the book.

Here is an example of a tree showing the hierarchical structure of the sentence Uruguay won the game:

12.

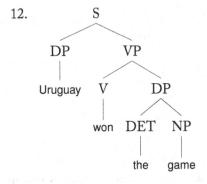

We build such a tree by composing its parts, i.e., elementary trees. In order to determine what the elementary trees are, we have to take the extended projection of the lexical heads that occur in the sentence. For the proper name Uruguay, the elementary tree is a determiner phrase (DP) projection without any arguments:

13.

The transitive verb to win selects two arguments: a subject and an object determiner phrase. In order to comprise the lexical item wins as well as both its arguments in one elementary tree, it has to be more complex, actually spanning the whole sentence:

14.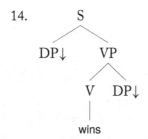

We write DP decorated with an arrow ↓ to indicate a *substitution node*, i.e., a place for substituting a tree with a DP root note.

Substitution is an operation that replaces a substitution node X ↓ in one tree with another tree with root node label X. For example, since the elementary verb tree has a substitution node DP↓ and the tree for Uruguay has a root node DP, we can substitute the former for the latter:

15.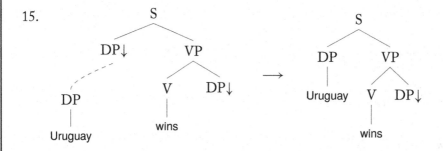

The object DP the game consists of two lexical items, the determiner the and the noun game. Assuming that the determiner selects for a noun, we have two elementary trees—a complex one for the determiner the and a simple one for the noun game—which combine to a DP by substitution:

16.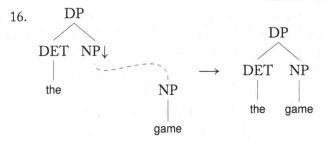

Finally, we can substitute the resulting DP tree into the still empty object slot of the verb tree.

The kind of elementary trees we have seen so far are called *initial trees*. It turns out that with these trees and the substitution operation we cannot yet cover all structures arising in language. Consider, for example, the sentence Uruguay wins the game easily.

17.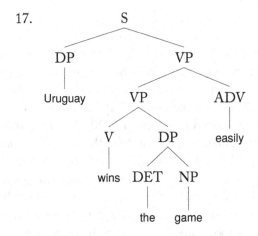

What kind of elementary tree would we need for the adverb easily in order to get the above structure? It should, in our case, modify the verb phrase and thus have a structure like the following:

18.   VP
       ╱╲
    VP↓ ADV
          |
        easily

However, this tree cannot be substituted into the verb tree, nor can the verb tree (which has a root node S) be substituted into this tree. So, in order to expand the VP with the adverb modification, we need a different operation, i.e., *adjunction*, which replaces an internal node with a tree.

Adjunction applies to a so-called *auxiliary tree* with a root C and a *foot node* $C*$ (where C is any syntactic category), and a tree with a matching node of category C, onto which the auxiliary tree is grafted. For example, the adjunction tree for easily looks exactly like the substitution tree above, just with a foot node VP* instead of the substitution node VP ↓. Since the verb tree has an interval VP-node, we can adjoin the adjunction tree to it:

19.

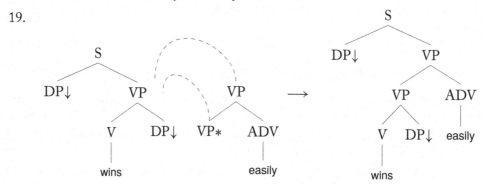

Substituting the DP-arguments proceeds as before. The result of such a derivation, i.e., a sequence of rule applications, is a so-called *derived tree*. Since there are usually several ways of composing one sentence, the derived tree does not always suffice to determine how it was constructed. Therefore it is important to also keep the history of which elementary trees were combined and in which way. *Derivation trees* uniquely specify such a history. For example, one derivation tree for the sentence No team wins easily is given in 20a; the resulting derived tree is given in 20c. The derivation tree is usually presented in a much more compact format, as given in 20b. The nodes *win*, *no*, etc. stand for the corresponding trees, and the hierarchy indicates that the tree corresponding to the daughter node was substituted (solid line) or adjoined (dashed line) into the tree corresponding to the mother node, where the number specifies the exact position (e.g., the node) of the mother node into which the tree was inserted. This number is defined quite straightforwardly: 0 denotes the root node, n is the n-th daughter of the root node, $i.j$ is the j-th daughter of the i-th daughter of the root node, and so on.

20.   (a)

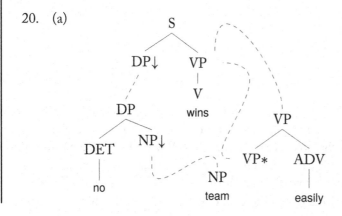

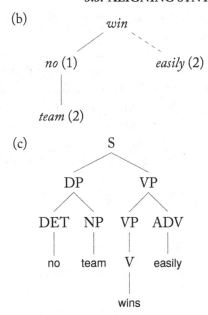

Derivation trees are the structures relevant for compositional semantic interpretation: When we pair syntactic and semantic representations, we will also pair syntactic and semantic operations, i.e., for every substitution and adjunction of two trees, there will be a corresponding semantic composition operation that combines the corresponding semantic representations.

Finally, let us look at *Lexicalized Tree Adjoining Grammar* (LTAG) [Schabes, 1990]. Lexicalized grammars assume that each atomic element or structure is associated with a lexical item. With respect to TAG, this means that elementary trees have to be associated with at least one lexical element, i.e., contain at least one leaf node labled with a non-empty terminal symbol, the *anchor*.

The lexicalization of grammars has formal significance, because it ensures that for any (finite) sentence there are only finitely many possible ways to compose it, such that the problem of recognizing whether a sentence is generated by the grammar is decidable. Also, it instantiates the view that syntactic rules are not completely separated from lexical items. An LTAG grammar consists of a lexicon that associates each lexical item with a finite number of elementary trees of which it is the anchor, together with the two syntactic rules of substitution and adjunction for combining trees.

3.3 ALIGNING SYNTACTIC REPRESENTATIONS TO AN ONTOLOGY

What does it mean to align an LTAG grammar to an ontology? In order to answer this question, recall the view on grammar that we introduced in the beginning of the chapter, especially the point that every basic syntactic element, i.e., every elementary tree, is associated with a meaning.

So far, we have not yet defined what meanings look like but intuitively we want meanings to refer to concepts, properties and individuals in our ontology.

That is, every elementary tree should be coupled with a meaning that refers to an ontology class, relation or entity. Now let us consider a specific example: The soccer ontology that we built in the previous chapter contains a relation `atMinute`, about which we can talk saying that some goal was scored in the 90th minute, some red card was issued in the 47th minute, and so on. In order to specify an LTAG that allows us to derive such statements, we would decompose the prepositional phrase into its parts, for example specifying the following elementary trees (the preposition tree could also be modifying an NP instead of a VP, of course, in order to derive noun phrases like the goal in the 90th minute):

21.

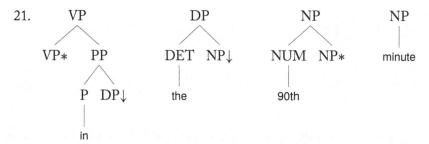

Abstracting from the exact numeral used, the meaning of the resulting prepositional phrase should correspond to the relation `atMinute`. Now what are the meanings of the elementary trees? According to our view of grammar, they should be meanings that all contribute to the meaning of the whole prepositional phrase. So what are the meaning parts of the relation `atMinute`? Since it is an atomic relation symbol, it does not have any parts. So it actually does not make sense to decompose the prepositional phrase syntactically, because we cannot assign meanings to its parts. The whole prepositional phrase (modulo the numeral) corresponds to one atomic element on the semantic side, so it should also be one atomic element on the syntactic side. This amounts to assuming the following elementary tree, which is then coupled with a meaning representing the relation `atMinute`:

22.

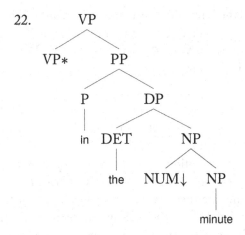

Recall Frank's constraint on elementary trees: Every elementary tree consists of the extended projection of a single lexical head. This is different now; elementary trees can be bigger, they can subsume several lexical heads, in our case in, the and minute. This is crucial for our approach. It means that we differ from the traditional approach in that we do not build elementary trees around single lexical items but rather around verbalizations of ontological concepts. So the size of elementary trees is partly imposed by the underlying ontology. We therefore reformulate Frank's constraint on elementary trees as follows.

Ontology-based elementary trees. *An elementary tree spans the extended projections of all lexical items that are required to verbalize a single ontology concept.*

This way we ensure that every basic syntactic element can be coupled with an ontology-based semantic representation. So let us now turn to what semantic representations are.

3.4   SEMANTIC REPRESENTATIONS: DRT

As formal representations of the meaning of natural language expressions, we exploit an extension of *Discourse Representation Structures* (DRSs). But before we turn to what they are, let us briefly think about what we want meaning representations to capture. First of all, they have to represent the content of a natural language expression or sentence, of course—in our case more specifically the content with regard to the underlying ontology. Second, a meaning representation should capture the semantic argument structure of the meaning of an expression and its relation to the syntactic argument structure of that expression. Consider, for example, the verb to win, as in my team won this game. In this example, the verb is used transitively, i.e., it has two syntactic arguments, a subject (my team) and a direct object (this game). As meaning we would want the relation winner, which has two semantic arguments, that is a subject (some game or tournament) and an object (the team that won). The semantic representation should tell us that winner is a binary relation with such two arguments. In addition it should contain information about the argument mapping, in particular that the semantic subject corresponds to the syntactic object, and the semantic object corresponds to the syntactic subject. This captures, for instance, the fact that the tripel in 23 can be verbalized as Uruguay won the World Cup final but not as The World Cup final won Uruguay. We will see how to accomplish this in more detail later in this chapter.

23. `soccer:WorldCupFinal1930 soccer:winner soccer:Uruguay` .

Thirdly, a semantic representation should capture different interpretation possibilities of an expression. We will postpone a discussion of this until Chapter 7.

Discourse Representation Structures (DRS) are representations from *Discourse Representation Theory* (DRT), which was developed by Hans Kamp [Kamp, 1981] and Uwe Reyle [Kamp and Reyle, 1993]. DRT is one member of a family of semantic theories that were developed for the interpretation of whole discourses instead of single, isolated sentences, mainly in order to deal with sentence-spanning phenomena such as anaphora. For an overview of such *dynamic semantics* see van Eijck and Visser [2012] or Dekker [2011]. The main idea behind having a dynamic semantic theory is that each sentence of a discourse is interpreted in the context of all preceding sentences, and furthermore updates the context with its content, yielding a new context in which subsequent sentences are interpreted. In DRT, content as well as context are represented by DRSs.

A DRS consists of two parts: a set of *reference markers* (or *discourse referents*), which represent the entities that a discourse is about, and a set of *conditions*, which specify properties of and relations among those entities. A simple example is the DRS given in 24b, representing the meaning of 24a.

24.   (a)   A player scored a penalty kick.

(b)

$x\,y$
$\text{player}(x)$
$\text{penaltykick}(y)$
$\text{score}(x, y)$

(c) $\exists x \exists y\, (\text{player}(x) \wedge \text{penaltykick}(y) \wedge \text{score}(x, y))$

The DRS contains two reference markers, x and y, and conditions that specify that x is a player, y is a penalty kick, and x stands in the relation of scoring with y. The reference markers in the top part of the DRS are interpreted as existentially quantified variables in first-order logic, and the bottom part is interpreted as the conjunction of all conditions. More specifically, the DRS in 24b is equivalent to the first-order formula in 24c. So the DRS can be viewed as a representation of the situation that the simple discourse in 24a describes: It contains at least two individuals that correspond to the markers x and y, and that satisfy the conditions, i.e., the individual corresponding to x is in the extension of `player`, the individual corresponding to y is in the extension of `penaltykick`, and the pair of both is in the extension of `score`.

In fact, the expressive power of DRT is the same as that of first-order logic. Moreover, they are intertranslatable: It is possible (and even quite straightforward) to translate every DRS into an equivalent first-order logical formula and vice versa. That is, in terms of truth conditions DRT does not add anything to first-order logic; rather it differs in the way it arrives at this expressivity. In DRT, the way the representations are built reflects the idea of a dynamic context change, and this context change is exploited for instance for the treatment of anaphora. For example, if a second sentence like He was nervous is added to 24a, as in 25a, the DRS given in 24b is extended with the content of that sentence. The added second sentence is thus interpreted in the context of the first one. The resulting DRS could look like 25b, containing the content of the first sentence plus the information that there is a new entity that is talked about, u, corresponding to the pronoun he, that this entity was nervous, and that it refers back to the entity x, i.e., to the player. The latter is of course not necessary; he could also refer to someone else, but the DRS in 25b captures the interpretation that takes a player and he to be coreferent.

25. (a) A player scored a penalty kick. He was nervous.

(b)

$x\,y\,u$
player(x)
penaltykick(y)
score(x, y)
nervous(u)
$u = x$

We will not worry about the mechanisms of anaphora resolution in this book, but the example gives you a first idea of the kind of phenomena that DRT was developed for.

The DRS conditions we have seen so far were simple unary and binary predicates. However, DRS conditions can also be more complex; we will see examples in the Appendix 3.7 below, when looking at quantifiers and negation. For the purposes of the book, however, the machinery we have so far suffices. We will therefore keep the examples throughout the book as well as the representations and definitions needed for them as simple as possible. So far, a discourse representation structure (DRS) for us therefore consists of:

- a finite set of *referent markers* (the *discourse universe*)

- a finite set of conditions, which are one of the following:

   - *atoms* are predicate constants applied to a list of referent markers
   - a *link* is an expression of form $x = y$, where x and y are referent markers

We can specify a standard, static model-theoretic interpretation of the well-formed DRSs in terms of truth and reference by means of *embeddings*, which are partial functions from the set of referent markers to the domain of the model, such that all conditions are satisfied. Another way of specifying an interpretation of DRT, which is closer to the original dynamic nature of DRT, is by specifying a dynamic semantics of DRSs in terms of total embeddings called *contexts*, where DRS conditions are (static) tests on contexts, while DRSs themselves are (dynamic) update operations on contexts. We skip the details of both the model-theoretic and the dynamic semantics of DRT, as they are not crucial to the book, and refer the interested reader to works cited in Section 3.8 below.

3.5   ALIGNING SEMANTIC REPRESENTATIONS TO AN ONTOLOGY

For the examples in the previous section, we constructed meaning representations that were very close to the syntactic structure of the natural language expression. For example, the sentence 26a could have a corresponding semantic representation as in 26b. This, however, does not match the domain ontology we have in mind. More specifically, our soccer ontology does not contain binary relations from and score. So what we actually want to construct are meaning representations that use predicates that are aligned to the underlying ontology, in our case a DRS like in 26c, expressing that there was a soccer action by a player playing for Uruguay that led to a goal. We use the prefix soccer to refer to our soccer ontology.

26.   (a)   A player from Uruguay scored a goal.

(b)

$x\,y$
player(x)
from$(x, \text{uruguay})$
goal(y)
score(x, y)

(c)

$x\,y\,z$
soccer:Player(x)
soccer:Goal(y)
soccer:SoccerAction(z)
soccer:byPlayer(z, x)
soccer:leadsTo(z, y)
soccer:playsFor$(x, \text{soccer:Uruguay})$

In order to arrive at meaning representations that are aligned to an ontology, we construct DRSs using the same vocabulary as the ontology, such that every non-logical constant, i.e., predicate or individual constant, corresponds to an ontology concept or entity. Specifically, we assume for every ontology class a corresponding unary predicate constant, e.g., Player, for every ontology property a binary predicate constant, e.g., playsFor, and for every individual in the ontology a corresponding individual constant, e.g., Uruguay.

The main challenge is to pair syntactic and semantic representation in a way that allows us to have such a correspondence. For example, the preposition from should be paired with a semantic representation using the predicate playsFor. This pairing is the subject of the next section.

3.6   FROM DRT TO DUDES: PAIRING SYNTACTIC AND SEMANTIC REPRESENTATIONS

Now that we have syntactic and semantic representations in place, we want to pair them, so that the processes of building a complex syntactic and semantic representation of a sentence can work in parallel. As an example, consider the following sentence:

27. Uruguay won against Argentina.

On the basis of the ontology-based syntactic and semantic representations we have been building in the previous sections, the building blocks of this sentence are two individuals Uruguay and Argentina, and the relation won against. The elementary trees and their corresponding DRSs are the following:

28. (a)

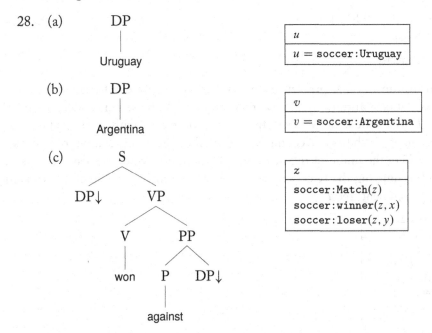

We have already seen how to combine these elementary trees into a complex sentence tree. But when thinking about the parallel semantic construction, we stumble upon two problems:

- What exactly is the combination of two DRSs?

- How does the interpretation process know that the interpretation of the subject DP corresponds to x, while the interpretation of the object DP corresponds to y, in the DRS for won against?

We will first address the second problem. The answer is quite simple: This is lexical knowledge that needs to be encoded in the representations. This requires an extension of the LTAG trees, namely a labeling of the substitution nodes, so that we can refer to them and thereby distinguish between, for example, subject and object DP node. The tree for won against would then look as in 29. Furthermore, we need to encode in the semantic representation that the interpretation of DP_1 is unified with x and the interpretation of DP_2 is unified with y. We do this by extending the DRS with a set of pairs of LTAG tree node labels and variables, as in 29.

29.

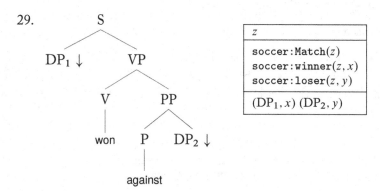

Now we can turn to the first problem mentioned above: What exactly is the combination of these representations? Intuitively, we want to end up with the sentence meaning in 30, so whenever a tree T with root node N is substituted in another tree with a substitution node $N \downarrow$, the interpretation of which has a selection pair (N, v), then the interpretations of both trees are combined by i) taking the union of the universes, the conditions and all selection pairs except for (N, v), and ii) unifying the selection variable v and the main variable of the semantic representation of the argument tree T.

30.

$z\ x\ y$
soccer:Match(z)
soccer:winner(z, x)
$x =$ soccer:Uruguay
soccer:loser(z, y)
$y =$ soccer:Argentina

But how does the interpretation process know which variables from the semantic representations of the DPs to unify with x or y? In our example this is trivial because there is only one (u in the meaning representation of Uruguay, and v in the one of Argentina), but we could also have a complex DP like a team with an excellent goalkeeper, which would contain a universe with two referent markers, one for the team and one for the goalkeeper. In that case we need to specify that it is the team referent that is unified, not the goalkeeper. So we have to add this information to the DRS in the form of one *distinguished* or *main* referent marker.

Adding a distinguished referent marker as well as selection pairs to DRSs, we arrive at semantic representations that contain information about how they can be combined with other representations. We call them DUDES, which stands for *Dependency-based Underspecified Discourse Representation Structures* [Cimiano, 2009], although they are not full-fledged DUDES yet. We will talk about their underspecification mechanism when adding quantifiers in Section 3.7. For most examples in the book, however, this machinery will not be necessary; we therefore use a simplified definition of DUDES.

Definition 3.1   DUDES (simplified)   A DUDES is a triple (v, D, S), where

- $v \in U$ is a referent marker (the distinguished or main variable),

- $D = (U, C)$ is a DRS with a discourse universe U and a set of conditions C, and

- S is a set of selection pairs of the form (N, v), where N is a LTAG tree node label and v is a referent marker.

Throwing in some syntactic sugar, the atomic semantic representations for the example Uruguay won against Argentina now appear as follows, where the left-most, boxed referent marker is the distinguished one:

31. (a)

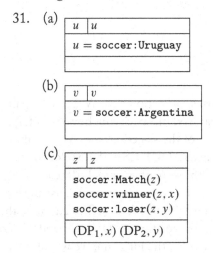

(b)

(c)

To formally capture the combination of DUDES, we define a semantic operation that specifies how to combine two DUDES when the corresponding trees are combined via substitution.

Definition 3.2   Semantic operation corresponding to substitution   When a tree with root N and an interpretation (v_1, D_1, S_1) is substituted in another tree with a substitution node $N \downarrow$ and an interpretation (v_2, D_2, S_2) with a selection pair $(N, v) \in S_2$, then the interpretation of the resulting tree is $(v_2, D_1[v_1 := v_2] \cup D_2, (S_1 \cup S_2) \backslash (N, v))$, where $\backslash$ is set subtraction, $D_1[v_1 := v_2]$ is like D_1 except that all occurrences of v_1 are substituted by v_2, and the union of two DRSs is the union of their universes and the union of their conditions: $(U_1, C_1) \cup (U_2, C_2) = (U_1 \cup U_2, C_1 \cup C_2)$.

This definition implicitly assumes an initial renaming of variables, if necessary, such that the set of variables used in the two DRSs are distinct.

The case of adjunction is very similar, we just do not have substitution nodes and selection pairs but simply unify the two interpretations.

Definition 3.3   Semantic operation corresponding to adjunction   When a tree with root N and an interpretation (v_1, D_1, S_1) is adjoined in another tree with an adjunction node $N*$ and interpretation (v_2, D_2, S_2), then the interpretation of the resulting tree is $(v_2, D_1[v_1 := v_2] \cup D_2, S_1 \cup S_2)$.

Combining the DUDES in 31 following these definitions yields the desired DUDES representation in 32. Note that the order of combination does not play a role—either combining 31c first with 31b and then combining the result with 31a or vice versa will give the same result.

32.

z	$z\ x\ y$
soccer:Match(z)	
soccer:winner(z, x)	
soccer:loser(z, y)	
x = soccer:Uruguay	
y = soccer:Argentina	

The rationale behind selection pairs is that a tree with substitution node $N \downarrow$ will be paired with a DUDES that contains a corresponding selection pair (N, v), specifying how the interpretation of the substituted tree unifies with the interpretation of the selecting tree. As a result, the interpretation of syntactically complete sentences always yields a DUDES with no selection pairs, and the semantics of this resulting DUDES is the same as the semantics of its DRS component.

In case a DUDES represents the semantic interpretation of a sentence, we will usually leave out the distinguished referent marker (for example z in the DUDES in 32). The reason is that these referent markers are used for the sentence-internal composition of DUDES and are not needed anymore once this composition is finished. Of course, in the long run, we will also want to compose sentence interpretations into interpretations of texts or dialogues. But in this case the referent markers we currently have are actually not enough. Rather we would need event variables that capture the event a sentence describes (for an overview of event semantics see Maienborn [2011]). Here is why. In the case of 32, the distinguished referent is the match z, which means that the sentence Uruguay won against Argentina describes a match. Arguably, a match is an event, so this seems fine. But the match actually differs from the event of Uruguay winning against Argentina. This becomes clear when considering modifiers. In Uruguay won easily, for example, the adverb easily does not modify the match, as it was not the match that was easy (certainly not for the other team), but the winning was. And it becomes even clearer when you take an example like Uruguay dominated the match and modify it, as in Uruguay dominated the match early. Again, it was not the match that was early but the dominating.

Currently, the ontology we assume does not allow us to express events and event modifications. Therefore we sidestep the issue of composing sentence interpretations.

3.7   QUANTIFIERS AND NEGATION

So far the DRS components of DUDES contained only simple predicates as conditions. However, DRS conditions need to be more complex in order to be able to represent scope-taking elements such as quantifiers and negation.

Let us first consider quantifiers. Up to now, DRSs only contained entities and predicates over those entities, but quantificational noun phrases, like every player or no team, do not refer to particular entities. Even assuming that they indicate the quantity of something, e.g., all players or the empty set of teams, does not seem right, as it is not quantities that get predicated over, e.g., it is not the empty set of teams that has certain properties. Rather, quantifiers relate sets. To give an intuition for this, consider the examples in 33.

33.   (a) [$_{NP}$ Some [$_N$ team]] [$_{VP}$ reached the finals].

    (b) [$_{NP}$ Every [$_N$ team]] [$_{VP}$ reached the finals].

    (c) [$_{NP}$ No [$_N$ team]] [$_{VP}$ reached the finals].

The quantifiers some, every and no relate the noun denotation, i.e., the set of teams, call it N, with the denotation of the VP, i.e., the set of entities that reached the finals, call it V. Now, the quantifier some expresses that the sets N and V have at least one element in common, i.e., $N \cap V \neq \emptyset$. The quantifier no, on the other hand, expresses that none of the members of N is in V, i.e., $N \cap V = \emptyset$. And the quantifier every expresses that all members of N are also in V, i.e., $N \subseteq V$ or $N \setminus V = \emptyset$.

Quantifier denotations are represented as complex DRS conditions called *duplex conditions*, which introduce subordinated DRSs and mirror the idea of relating sets. Their general form is the one in 34a, its instantiation in the case of 33c is given in 34b.

34.   (a)

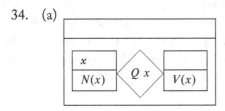

(b)

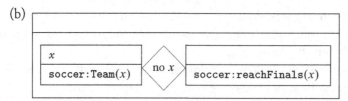

The left-hand side DRS is usually called *restrictor*, and the right-hand side is called *scope*.

As a rule of thumb, every meaning contribution of the noun denotation, e.g., denotations of modifiers or relative clauses, will end up in the restrictor, while all meaning contributions of the verb phrase will end up in the scope. This is illustrated in the following example.

35. (a) No nervous player scores a penalty kick.

(b)

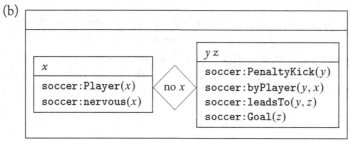

Exercise 3.4 Quantifiers and the resulting duplex conditions can be nested. What would a DRS for the sentence No player who misses all penalty kicks is happy look like?

In addition to quantifiers, negation is also a scope-taking element and thus is expressed in DRT as a complex condition, more specifically a negated DRS. A basic example is given in 36.

36. (a) A lazy player is not excellent.

(b)

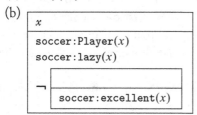

Now you might ask: Why not just negate simple conditions and express the negation in 36 as the simple condition $\neg\, \mathtt{excellent}(x)$? The reason is that the semantic content that is negated might be more complex and might even state the existence of some specified discourse referent. An example of this is given in 37. The sentence in 37a expresses the fact that for some excellent team there is no coach related to it. The negation of the existence of such a coach is captured by negating the embedded DRS (recall that the reference markers in this DRS are interpreted as existentially quantified variables).

37. (a) Some excellent team does not have a coach.

(b)

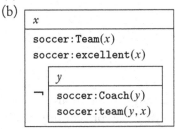

Exercise 3.5   Having a negation operator provides us with another way of representing the meaning of the following sentence from Exercise 3.4 above: No player who misses all penalty kicks is happy. What would a DRS look like that uses negation instead of a quantified duplex condition?

Finally, we might add disjunction as an operator for connecting two DRSs to form a complex condition, as exemplified in 38.

38. (a) An excellent player is either talented or trained.

(b)

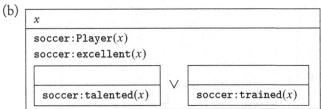

Note that adding conjunction as an additional operator would be redundant, as the list of conditions in a DRS is interpreted conjunctively already.

Now that we added complex conditions to DRSs, what does that mean for the DUDES and their semantic composition? That we need more than we have so far becomes clear when thinking about how to construct a meaning representation for a sentence like 39a. It is composed of two noun phrases, Pelé with the meaning given in 39b and every penalty kick with the meaning given in 39c, and the transitive verb score with the meaning given in 39d.

39. (a) Pelé scored every penalty kick.

(b)

(c)

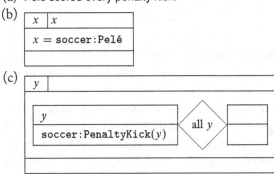

(d)

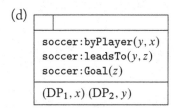

$$\text{soccer:byPlayer}(y, x)$$
$$\text{soccer:leadsTo}(y, z)$$
$$\text{soccer:Goal}(z)$$
$$(DP_1, x)\ (DP_2, y)$$

When combining the DUDES in 39c–39d, the meaning contributions of score and Pelé need to go into the scope of the duplex condition in order to yield the correct truth conditions. But so far we have no way of specifying this; according to our semantic composition rule in Section 3.6 above, the content of the DRS components in the DUDES 39b and 39d would simply be added as further conditions to the overall DRS.

Even more, a sentence like 40a is ambiguous w.r.t. quantifier scope. It means either that for most coaches x it is the case that x respects all players, represented in 40b, or that for all players y, most coaches respect y, represented in 40c (leaving out the soccer prefix for space reasons).

40. (a) Most coaches respect all players.

(b)

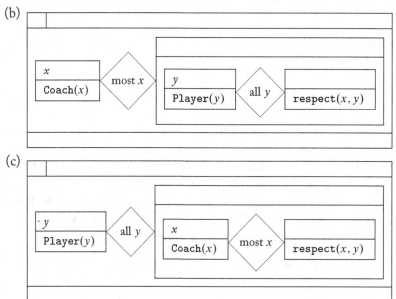

(c)

So in one case the meaning of x respect all players has to be in the scope of the quantifier most coaches x, and in the other case the meaning of most coaches respect y has to be in the scope of the quantifier all players y.

Such ambiguities also arise with other scope-taking elements, such as negation. The sentence 41a, for example, has two readings: Either it is not the case that all teams won the World Cup final (so there is at least one team that did not win it), as depicted in 41b, or for every team it is the case that it did not win the World Cup final (so no team won it), as depicted in 41c.

41.   (a) Every team did not win a World Cup final.

(b)

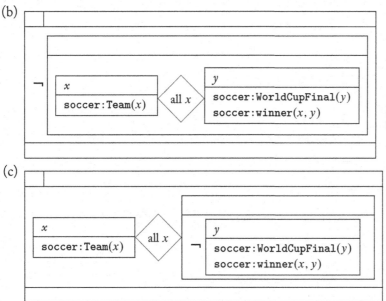

(c)

Again in one case the duplex condition introduced by every team is in the subordinated DRS introduced by negation, and in the other case the DRS introduced by negation is in the scope of the duplex condition.

In order to allow for a flexible composition of DUDES that captures such scope ambiguities, we exchange the DRSs that underlie our DUDES by UDRSs, *Underspecified Discourse Representation Structures*. Underspecified DRT [Reyle, 1993] is a variant of DRT that was developed in order to capture exactly such ambiguities. The main idea is to not unify DRSs as soon as they are composed, but to keep them in one underspecified representation that can then be resolved to different representations of the whole sentence. The underspecified sentence representation of 40a would look as in 42a, the underspecified representation of 41a as in 42b. They capture different orders of composing the parts into a DRS for the whole sentence. Depending on which order is chosen, one scope-taking element (i.e., quantifier or negation) gets scope over the other.

42.   (a)

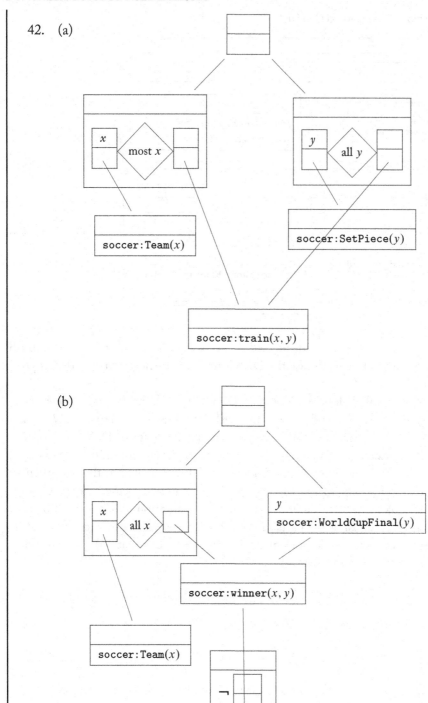

(b)

For our DUDES this means that, instead of having one DRS component, they now comprise a set of DRS components, which get labels so that we can properly refer to them, together with information about how they can be combined. This leads to the following more comprehensive definitions of DUDES:

Definition 3.6 DUDES   A DUDES is a quintuple (v, l, D, S, R), where

- v is a referent marker (the distinguished or main variable),

- l is a label (the distinguished or main label),

- D is a set of labeled DRSs of form $l : (U, C)$ with U a discourse universe and C a set of conditions,

- S is a set of selection pairs of the form (N, v, l), where N is an LTAG tree node label, v is a referent marker, and l is a label,

- R is a set of subordination relations as defined in Definition 3.7 below.

We will use variables $l, l', l_1, l_2, \ldots$ for labels. Subordination relations make use of these labels to express which DRS component is to be unified with which other one.

Definition 3.7 Subordination relation   A *subordination relation* is an expression of form $l < l'$, where l and l' are either atomic labels or results of the following functions:

- $\top_l$ returns the top component of the DRS labeled by l, i.e., that component D_1 with label l_1 such that there is no other component D_2 with label l_2 such that $l_1 < l_2$,

- $\bot_l$ returns the bottom component of the DRS labeled by l, i.e., that component D_1 with label l_1 such that there is no other component D_2 with label l_2 such that $l_2 < l_1$,

- res(l) returns the restrictor component of quantifier representations (and l in all other cases), and

- scope(l) returns the scope component of quantifier representations (and l in all other cases).

As an example, the DUDES for the quantifier every now looks as follows.

43.

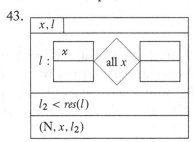

This means that the meaning contribution of the noun with which it is combined is going to be unified with the restrictor of the duplex condition. The combinatory potential that will give rise to scope ambiguities is part of the verb meaning. The transitive verb win, for example, has a DUDES as in 44a. For ease of understanding, one can read it as depicted in 44b. (As before, we leave out the distinguished referent marker.)

44.   (a)

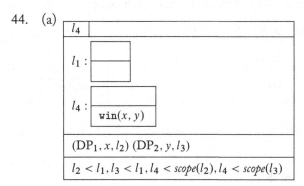

$$l_2 < l_1, l_3 < l_1, l_4 < scope(l_2), l_4 < scope(l_3)$$

(b)

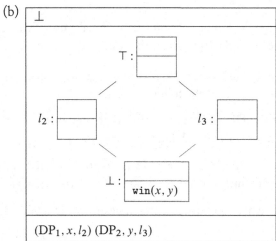

Finally we need to adapt our semantic composition operation to these new representations.

Definition 3.8   Semantic operation corresponding to substitution (adapted)   When a tree with root N and an interpretation $(v_1, l_1, D_1, S_1, R_1)$ is substituted in another tree with a substitution node $N_i \downarrow$ and an interpretation $(v_2, l_2, D_2, S_2, R_2)$ with a selection pair $(N_i, v, l) \in S_2$, then the interpretation of the resulting tree is $(v_2, l_2, D_1[v_1 := v_2][l_1 := l_2] \cup D_2, (S_1 \cup S_2)\backslash(N_i, v, l), R_1 \cup R_2)$.

The adaptation of the operation corresponding to adjunction is very similar.

Exercise 3.9 For the two example sentences above, repeated in 45, specify an LTAG tree and DUDES for every occurring lexical item, and construct the meaning representation of the whole sentence according to the definitions.

45. (a) Most teams train all set pieces.

   (b) Every team did not win the World Cup final.

3.8 FURTHER READING

TAGs were first introduced by Joshi et al. [1975] and Joshi [1985]. An overview of LTAGs can be found in the technical report by Joshi and Schabes [1991]. A semantics for LTAG based on labels and holes has been provided by Kallmeyer and Joshi [2003], one for feature-based TAG by Gardent and Kallmeyer [2003].

The basic ideas of dynamic semantics are described, e.g., by van Eijck and Visser [2012] and Dekker [2011]. Details on DRT, including an interpretation of DRSs, can be found in the DRT book [Kamp and Reyle, 1993] and several handbook articles [Kamp et al., 2011; van Eijck and Kamp, 1996]. Kamp's original 1981 paper on DRT is contained in a collection of seminal papers that shaped formal semantics [Portner and Partee, 2002]. DUDES were defined by Cimiano [2009]. They are based on Underspecified DRT [Reyle, 1993] and earlier work of Cimiano et al. [2007].

Readers especially interested in computational semantics will find plenty of fuel in the books by Blackburn and Bos [2005] and van Eijck and Unger [2010].

Finally, there is a wide range of linguistic formalisms that we could have built on for parsing and interpretation. One that we have explored for the ontology-based interpretation of natural language and found very suitable in this context is Grammatical Framework [Ranta, 2011]. Other relevant grammatical formalisms include Categorial Grammar [Moortgat, 1997; Steedman, 1996], Lexical Functional Grammar (LFG) [Kaplan and Bresnan, 1982] with, e.g., Glue Semantics and UDRT as semantic composition formalism [van Genabith and Crouch, 1999], and Head-driven Phrase Structure Grammar (HPSG) [Levine and Meurers, 2006] with Minimal Recursion Semantics (MRS) [Copestake et al., 2005] as semantic formalism of choice.

CHAPTER 4

Ontology Lexica

In the introduction we argued that the meaning of a certain word or lexical construction can be seen as specific to a given domain and ontology, as different ontologies make semantic distinctions at different levels of granularity. Thus, if we want to compute semantic representations that are specific for a given ontology, we need to specify how words or more complex syntactic constructions are interpreted with respect to the given ontological vocabulary.

Ideally, we would like to do so in a declarative fashion, abstracting from specific syntactic and semantic theories. The benefit of such theory-neutrality is that the declarative representation can then be translated into any grammatical formalism or semantic theory of our choice. Further, we would like to do this in such a way that the *ontology lexica* can be published on the web in a standard web format (e.g., RDF) and are linked to the original ontology, thus facilitating their discovery and reuse.

The *Lexicon Model for Ontologies*, or *lemon* for short, is such a model for specifying the lexicon-ontology interface, allowing one to state the meaning of lexical entries and constructions with respect to the vocabulary of a given ontology declaratively. In this chapter, we introduce the ideas behind *lemon* and the details of the model, discussing how the lexicon-ontology interface is specified for different open-class words, such as nouns, verbs and adjectives.

4.1 THE *LEMON* MODEL

The *lemon* model follows a principle that has been referred to as *semantics by reference* [McCrae et al., 2011] and states that the meaning of a lexical entry is specified by reference to a certain ontological class, property or individual. Thus, the semantic vocabulary used to represent the meaning of words corresponds to the vocabulary of the ontology.

The core of the *lemon* model is depicted in Figure 4.1, where arrows with filled heads represent properties and arrows with empty heads indicate subclasses and subproperties. It defines the following main entities:

- A *lexicon* is a set of lexical entries and is specific for a certain language. For each ontology, there can be many lexica for different languages.

- A *lexical entry* is either a word, phrase or particle.

- A *form* represents a surface realization of a given lexical entry, typically a written representation, but possibly also a phonetic one.

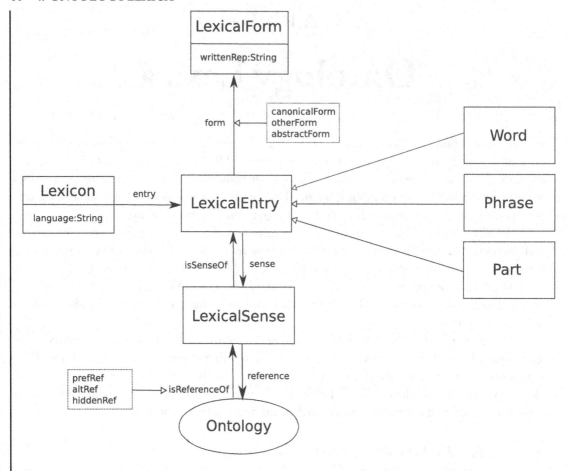

Figure 4.1: Core of the *lemon* model.

- A *reference* is an ontological entity, i.e., a class, a property or an individual, that represents the meaning of a lexical entry with respect to the ontology.

- A *lexical sense* is a reification of the meaning of an entry and thus allows for the attachment of usage-related constraints or other pragmatic information onto the pair consisting of a lexical entry and a reference.

In addition, *lemon* contains several modules for describing different dimensions of the lexicon-ontology interface. Of particular interest in the case of ontology-based interpretation is the *syntax and mapping module*, which describes the connection between syntactic constructions and semantic predicates. It defines the following extra classes:

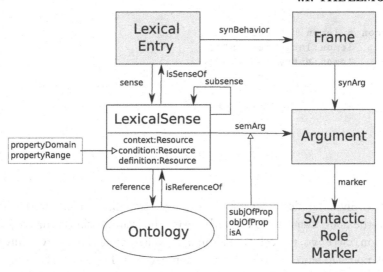

Figure 4.2: The syntax and mapping model of *lemon*.

- A *frame* represents one syntactic frame in which the lexical entry can occur, in particular making the syntactic arguments explicit (see below).

- An *argument* represents a syntactic argument of a specific frame in which the lexical entry occurs.

- A *syntactic role marker* is either a lexical entry (generally an adposition) or a syntactic annotation (generally a grammatical case).

Further modules of *lemon* describe inter-lexical and intra-lexical linking, syntactic categories, morphology and syntactic decomposition (for an overview see the *lemon* cookbook[1]).

In order to illustrate how the *lemon* vocabulary is used, we proceed now by examples, showing how the model allows for the representation of different aspects of the meaning of a word with respect to a given ontology. All our examples will be given in Turtle RDF syntax. For a brief explanation of Turtle, please see Section 1.4 in the Introduction.

The following shows how a lexicon together with a number of lexical entries would be represented. It shows a lexicon for the English language for our soccer ontology containing lexical entries for the nouns team, match and goal as well as the verb to win, and others. The first line indicates that identities without a namespace are IDs in the current document.

```
45. @prefix : <#> .
    @prefix lemon: <http://www.lemon-model.net/lemon#> .
```

---

[1]http://lemon-model.net/cookbook.html

```
:lexicon a lemon:Lexicon ;
         lemon:language "en" ;
         lemon:entry :team,
                     :match,
                     :goal,
                     :striker,
                     :win,
                     :play,
                     ...   .
```

The following example shows how we can associate different (written) forms to one lexical entry, e.g., to the noun team and to the verb to win. The example shows that lexical entries have a so-called canonicalForm, typically the lemma, as well as otherForms, typically inflected forms. We use blank nodes to represent the forms for compactness. In practice, however, it is highly recommended that every element of the model be assigned a URI to make referencing and querying simpler.

```
46. @prefix : <#> .
    @prefix lemon: <http://www.lemon-model.net/lemon#> .

    :team a lemon:Word ;
          lemon:canonicalForm [ lemon:writtenRep "team"@en  ] ;
          lemon:otherForm     [ lemon:writtenRep "teams"@en ] .

    :win  a lemon:Word ;
          lemon:canonicalForm [ lemon:writtenRep "win"@en   ] ;
          lemon:otherForm     [ lemon:writtenRep "wins"@en  ] ;
          lemon:otherForm     [ lemon:writtenRep "won"@en   ] ;
          lemon:otherForm     [ lemon:writtenRep "winning"@en ] .
```

Keep in mind that the identifiers :team and :win here represent lexical entries, i.e., are not the same as the ontology elements soccer:Team and soccer:winner. Up to now they are not even related, although our goal is to do that, of course.

Also note that we have not provided any additional information about the properties of the different written forms. In particular, we have so far not stated that teams is the plural of team, and that wins is the first person singular present tense of win, etc. For this, we would need additional vocabulary that is not part of the *lemon* model proper. We will see below how such additional properties can be defined by using an external ontology of linguistic categories.

We can also represent lexical entries graphically. For the above entry for the verb to win in 46 this would look as follows:

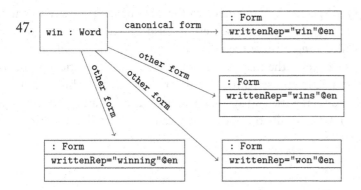

47.

The `reference` property allows us to relate a lexical entry to a symbol that represents its meaning in a given ontology. This is shown by the following code.

```
48. :team lemon:sense [ lemon:reference soccer:Team ].
    :win  lemon:sense [ lemon:reference soccer:winner ].
```

Graphically it can be depicted as follows:

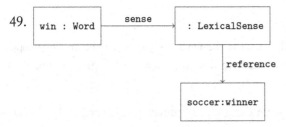

49.

We now give an example of how to represent the syntactic behavior of a lexical entry using a `Frame` that has a certain number and type of syntactic arguments. We consider the case of the verb to win and its transitive usage, i.e., someone wins something.

```
50. @prefix : <#> .
    @prefix soccer: <http://www.ontosem.net/ontologies/soccer#> .

    :win a lemon:Word ;
        lemon:canonicalForm [ lemon:writtenRep "win"@en  ] ;
        lemon:otherForm     [ lemon:writtenRep "wins"@en ] ;

        lemon:synBehavior   [ lemon:synArg :win_arg1 ;
                              lemon:synArg :win_arg2 ] ;

        lemon:sense         [ lemon:reference soccer:winner;
                              lemon:subjOfProp :win_arg2 ;
                              lemon:objOfProp  :win_arg1 ] .
```

The meaning of the lexical entry is specified by reference to the ontological property `winner`. A property in the ontology has a semantic subject—sometimes also called *domain*—as well as a semantic object—sometimes called *range*. These are referred to through the *lemon* properties `subjOfProp` and `objOfProp`, respectively. The mapping from syntactic to semantic arguments is then realized by unifying the syntactic and semantic arguments. Technically, this is done by using the same identifier/URI for the semantic and syntactic arguments (win_arg1 and win_arg, respectively, in our example above). Graphically the above entry can be depicted as follows:

51.

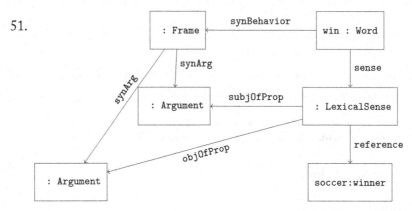

Exercise 4.1   Model graphically the lexical entry for the verb to support as used in Peter supports Portsmouth FC as mapping to the property `hasFan` with domain `Team` and range `Person`.

Exercise 4.2   Write down the entry you have designed graphically in Exercise 4.1 in Turtle format.

This in essence represents the core of the *lemon* model. In what follows we demonstrate how an external linguistic ontology can be used to represent additional properties of lexical entries, forms, syntactic behavior and syntactic arguments, such as the particular type of arguments that a certain lexical entry requires (e.g., direct and indirect objects), their grammatical function, the type of a frame (e.g., intransitive, transitive) or which type of written form we are referring to (e.g., 3rd person singular present tense).

4.2   USING LEXINFO AS LINGUISTIC ONTOLOGY

The LexInfo[2] ontology extends the *lemon* model with more than 600 specific linguistic categories. It can be used to add properties to different forms of a lexical entry. Consider the case of the verb to win. We can specify different written forms together with information about person, number, tense and the like as follows:

[2]The LexInfo ontology can be downloaded at http://www.lexinfo.net/ontology/2.0/lexinfo.

```
52.  :win a lemon:Word ;
         lexinfo:partOfSpeech lexinfo:verb ;

     lemon:canonicalForm [ lemon:writtenRep "win"@en ;
                           lexinfo:tense lexinfo:present ] ;

     lemon:otherForm     [ lemon:writtenRep "wins"@en ;
                           lexinfo:tense lexinfo:present;
                           lexinfo:person lexinfo:thirdPerson;
                           lexinfo:number lexinfo:singular ] .

     lemon:otherForm     [ lemon:writtenRep "won"@en ;
                           lexinfo:tense lexinfo:past;
                           lexinfo:verbFormMood lexinfo:participle;
                           lexinfo:aspect lexinfo:perfective] .

     lemon:otherForm     [ lemon:writtenRep "winning"@en ;
                           lexinfo:verbFormMood lexinfo:gerundive ].
```

We can also use the LexInfo ontology to specify the type of linguistic frame, in the case of
to win a transitive verb frame, together with the type of syntactic arguments, here a subject and a
direct object:

```
53.  :win lemon:synBehavior [ a lexinfo:TransitiveFrame ;
                              lexinfo:subject       :arg1 ;
                              lexinfo:directObject :arg2 ] ;

     lemon:sense         [ lemon:reference soccer:winner;
                           lemon:subjOfProp :arg2 ;
                           lemon:objOfProp  :arg1 ] .
```

Note that the identifiers of the syntactic arguments, subject and directObject, and the semantic arguments, subjOfProp and objOfProp, are the same. In this way we specify that the
syntactic subject corresponds to the semantic object of the ontology relation (the winner), while
the syntactic object corresponds to the semantic subject (the thing that is won).

The graphical representation of the complete lexical entry for to win is depicted in Figure 4.3.

Exercise 4.3   Complete your entry for the verb supports by specifying the frame type and the
type of arguments using the LexInfo ontology.

Using the LexInfo categories has several advantages. First, LexInfo is an ontology and thus
allows for consistency checking and reasoning. Second, LexInfo is linked to several data category
repositories such as ISOcat [Kemps-Snijders et al., 2008], thus facilitating interoperability. Further, LexInfo is already used by many existing *lemon* models such as WordNet exports [McCrae

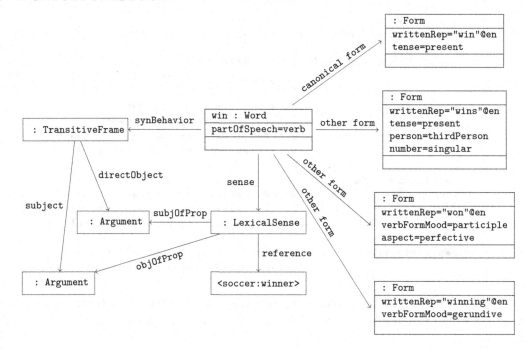

Figure 4.3: Graphical depiction of the lexical entry for the verb to win.

et al., 2012a] and Wiktionary [Chiarcos et al., 2012]. We give below the example of two data categories that are specified in LexInfo, `number` and `plural`, showing how they are linked to corresponding ISOcat categories:

```
54. @prefix lexinfo: <http://www.lexinfo.net/ontology/2.0/lexinfo> .
    @prefix dcr:     <http://www.isocat.org/ns/dcr.rdf#> .

    lexinfo:number a owl:ObjectProperty ;
        dcr:datcat <http://www.isocat.org/datcat/DC-1298> ;
        dcr:datcat <http://www.isocat.org/datcat/DC-251>   .

    lexinfo:plural a lexinfo:Number ;
        dcr:datcat <http://www.isocat.org/datcat/DC-1354> ;
        dcr:datcat <http://www.isocat.org/datcat/DC-253> .
```

Note that we use the property `datcat` to link to ISOcat data categories instead of standard OWL properties such as `equivalentProperty` as this is the practice recommended by the maintainers of the ISOcat repository (see Windhouwer and Wright [2012]).

4.3 MODELING WORD CLASSES IN *LEMON*

In this section, we look at what the entries for different syntactic categories look like in *lemon*, concentrating on the open-class syntactic categories: proper nouns, nouns, verbs, adjectives and adverbs. Proper nouns typically refer to individuals in the ontology, while nouns refer to either classes or properties. We will discuss different types of adjectives focusing in particular on intersective, scalar and property-modifying adjectives. For the sake of completeness we also discuss adverbs but in a rather superficial fashion. The main issue with adverbs is that they are not a homogenous category [Cinque, 1999]. In some cases they work analogously to adjectives, just modifying an adjective or verb instead of a noun. However, the representation of the semantics of adverbs very often requires spatio-temporal modeling, the discussion of which is beyond the scope of this chapter.

We will not consider prepositions here. Although it can be argued that they have a domain-independent meaning (see Chapter 7 for an account of their semantics), we concentrate on modeling the very specific meaning that they acquire in the context of a particular frame of a lexical entry, e.g., assigning a particular ontological role to the corresponding prepositional object. It is this frame-specific meaning of a preposition that is in many cases domain-specific and that will consequently be specified in a *lemon* lexicon.

In general, each lexical entry in a *lemon* lexicon has a number of syntactic arguments that map to semantic arguments of an ontological property or a more complex semantic frame. In general, we require that there is a one-to-one mapping between syntactic arguments subcategorized by a certain lexical entry and the set of semantic arguments specified in the lexical entry. For all lexical entries, we assume that there is a stereotypical usage or construction involving the lexical entry in which all syntactic arguments are actually realized. This is for instance the active indicative sentence for verbs (e.g., Peter admires Cantona) and a copula sentence for nouns (e.g., Peter is a goalkeeper). These stereotypical constructions essentially specify the syntax-semantics interface, but can be surface-realized in very different forms, e.g., as a passive (Cantona is admired by Peter) in the case of a verb or in a relative clause (who Peter admires) or in a topicalized form (Cantona, Peter admires). It is then the task of the grammar generation component to generate all these forms.

We do not consider closed-class parts of speech such as determiners and pronouns as their semantics is not specific to a particular domain ontology and they do not need to be represented in *lemon*. How the semantics of domain-independent expressions like determiners is captured in our approach will be discussed in Chapter 6.

4.3.1 PROPER NOUNS

Proper nouns always refer to an individual. Therefore, capturing the semantics of proper nouns is rather trivial in *lemon*. The reference is a URI representing the individual in question. We give two examples, one for a player and one for a team:

```
55. :Messi a lemon:LexicalEntry ;
        lexinfo:partOfSpeech lexinfo:properNoun ;
```

```
        lemon:canonicalForm [ lemon:writtenRep "Lionel Messi"@en] ;
        lemon:sense         [ lemon:reference soccer:LionelMessi] .

:Barcelona a lemon:LexicalEntry;
        lexinfo:partOfSpeech lexinfo:properNoun ;
        lemon:canonicalForm [ lemon:writtenRep "FC Barcelona"@en] ;
        lemon:sense         [ lemon:reference soccer:FCBarcelona] .
```

4.3.2   NOUNS

Typically, nouns denote classes, but in other cases they can also denote relations or properties. An example of a noun which clearly denotes a class is animal, while nouns that clearly denote a relation are for instance father or capital.

Class Nouns

In traditional accounts of formal semantics, nouns are understood as denoting a property, or to be precise, a set of objects having a certain property, e.g., the property of being a match, a striker, or a goal.

Typically, the semantics of nouns is modeled as a characteristic function for the set A in question, i.e., as a function $f_A(x)$ that returns true if $x \in A$ and false otherwise. One could thus say that in this representation there is a semantic argument, i.e., the x that is not saturated. As in *lemon* we assume that all semantic arguments need to be mapped to some syntactic argument that realizes it, we model class nouns as being stereotypically realized in a copula construction, where the copula subject provides the syntactic argument that is bound to the semantic argument x. Here is an example entry, verbalizing the noun striker:

```
56. :striker a lemon:Word ;
        lexinfo:partOfSpeech lexinfo:noun ;
        lemon:canonicalForm [ lemon:writtenRep "striker"@en ].

        lemon:synBehavior   [ a lexinfo:NounPredicateFrame ;
                              lemon:synArg :striker_arg ] ;

        lemon:sense         [ lemon:reference soccer:Striker ;
                              lemon:isA :striker_arg ] .
```

This entry makes explicit that the noun striker refers to the ontological class Striker and associates the semantic argument of the characteristic function of this class to the subject of the stereotypical realization of the noun as a copula construction, such as Peter is a striker.

There are other common nouns the semantics of which does not simply correspond to a named atomic class as in the examples above. An example of such a compound class is the concept *paternal grandfather*, which in many languages is expressed by a distinct word, e.g., farfar in Swedish (as opposed to morfar for *maternal grandfather*). In case the ontology in question does not introduce this concept *paternal/maternal grandfather*, we can introduce a corresponding new concept at the lexicon-ontology interface, i.e., in the lexicon, by using OWL axioms. In our case, the concept *paternal grandfather* could be defined as follows (recall the definition of $\mathcal{ALC}$ expressions on page 24):

57. `PaternalGrandfather` $\equiv \exists$ `hasChild.[Male` $\sqcap \exists$ `hasChild.Person]`

In practice there is no difference between simple classes like `Goal` and complex classes like `PaternalGrandfather`, except for their namespace. While the latter class physically belongs to the lexicon and is introduced to capture the semantics of farfar, conceptually it belongs to the ontology. So in a way we are extending the ontology, as the concept is assembled from the logical vocabulary defined in the ontology. One could even say that the concept already exists in the ontology, but simply has no name, i.e., has not been singled out as an atomic concept. In the lexicon we then introduce a name and directly lexicalize it.

Relational Nouns

Relational nouns are regarded as expressing a relation rather than a class (see de Bruin and Scha [1988]). Let us consider the example of the noun capital, which is seen traditionally as a relational noun as it relates a country and its main city. We can model the noun capital as relating to an object property `hasCapital` in some example ontology.

58.
```
: capital a lemon:Word ;
      lexinfo:partOfSpeech lexinfo:noun ;
      lemon:canonicalForm [ lemon:writtenRep "capital"@en ];

      lemon:synBehavior    [ a lexinfo:NounPredicateFrame;
                             lexinfo:copulativeArg     :capital_arg2;
                             lexinfo:possessiveAdjunct :capital_arg1 ];

      lemon:sense          [ lemon:reference onto:hasCapital;
                             lemon:subjOfProp  :capital_arg1;
                             lemon:objOfProp   :capital_arg2];
```

Here the syntactic behavior is specified as a `NounPredicateFrame` with two arguments. The first one is the *copulative argument* as in the case of class nouns. The second argument is a *possessive adjunct* the grammatical realization of which is language-specific. In English for instance, such possessive adjuncts are realized as a genitive or prepositional phrase with the preposition of. That is, capital prototypically occurs in sentences like the following ones:

59. (a) Berlin is the capital of Germany.

    (b) Berlin is Germany's capital.

    (c) The capital of Germany is Berlin.

    (d) Germany's capital is Berlin.

By means of the very general copulative argument and possessive adjunct, we can thus capture all these lexicalizations, as we assume that the semantic object (Berlin) can appear as a subject or an object, and we allow for both the genitive and the prepositional object realization of the semantic subject (Germany). While the usage of a possessive adjunct can be considered to be linguistically universal, it is necessary to write a frame to indicate that it is the lexicalization of a specific object property.

To consider a slightly more complex entry, let us consider the case of the noun coach which expresses a time-indexed person role (a common ontology design pattern described by Gangemi and Presutti [2009]) according to the following axiomatization:

60. CoachRole $\sqsubseteq$ TimeIndexedPersonRole
     CoachRole $\sqsubseteq$ $\exists$ forTeam.Team
     CoachRole $\sqsubseteq$ $\exists$ coach.Person
     CoachRole $\sqsubseteq$ $\exists$ during.TimeInterval

According to this modeling, the lexicon entry for coach would look as follows:

```
61.  :coach a lemon:Word ;
     lexinfo:partOfSpeech lexinfo:noun ;
     lemon:canonicalForm [ lemon:writtenRep "coach"@en ] ;

     lemon:synBehavior      [ a lexinfo:NounPPFrame ;
                             lexinfo:copulativeArg        :coach_arg1 ;
                             lexinfo:prepositionalObject :coach_arg2 ] ;

     lemon:sense            [ lemon:reference soccer:CoachRole.
                             lemon:isA :coach_role ] ;

                             lemon:subsense [
                             lemon:reference soccer:coach;
                             lemon:subjOfProp :coach_role;
                             lemon:objOfProp  :coach_arg1 ] ;

                             lemon:subsense [
                             lemon:reference soccer:forTeam;
                             lemon:subjOfProp :coach_role;
                             lemon:objOfProp  :coach_arg2 ] ] .

     :coach_arg2 lemon:marker :for .
```

Note that above we introduce complex senses that consist of several subsenses mapping each of the syntactic arguments (the copulative subject and the prepositional object) to the roles coach and forTeam of the time-index person role CoachRole.

4.3.3 VERBS

Verbs typically require a number of syntactic arguments. For instance, nearly all verbs require a subject. Transitive verbs, such as to admire, in addition require a direct object. In addition to a direct object, ditransitive verbs, such as to give, further require an indirect object. Verbs can also take other arguments marked with prepositions or further cases.

We will now illustrate how the ontology-specific semantics of verbs can be captured with *lemon*. We discuss three semantic categories of verbs that are typically distinguished in the literature: state verbs, event verbs and consequence verbs. State verbs describe a condition that holds over time. An example is the condition of being a player for a certain team, which is bound to a certain time interval over which this condition holds. An event verb describes something that happens in time and that involves some change of state, i.e., some effect on the world. An example is the event of scoring a goal, which has a culmination point (e.g., in the ball passing the goal line) that leads to a change in the scores. Consequence verbs rather refer to the consequence of a culminating state that a certain event has. An example for this would be the verb to win which rather refers to the final state of the game rather than to a particular event.

State Verbs

The actual semantics of a state verb depends on the ontological modeling in the ontology. In the simplest case, if the modeling ignores the temporal extension of the condition in question, the modeling can be as simple as claiming that the verb refers to a binary property in the ontology. In the case of the verbal construction to play for and assuming the existence of a property playsFor in the ontology, the modeling in *lemon* would look as follows:

```
62. :play a lemon:Word ;
        lexinfo:partOfSpeech lexinfo:verb ;
        lemon:canonicalForm [ lemon:writtenRep "play"@en ] ;

        lemon:synBehavior    [ rdf:type lexinfo:IntransitivePPFrame ;
                               lexinfo:subject            :play_arg1;
                               lexinfo:prepositionalObject :play_arg2 ] ;

        lemon:sense          [ lemon:reference soccer:playsFor ;
                               lemon:subjOfProp :play_arg1;
                               lemon:objOfProp  :play_arg2 ] .

    :play_arg2 lemon:marker :for .
```

This entry expresses that play is a verb that in this case, requires two arguments, a subject and a prepositional object marked by the preposition for. Semantically, it refers to the property playsFor, whereby the syntactic subject expresses the semantic subject of the property and the syntactic object expresses the semantic object of the property.

If the ontology models the temporal extension of the state, then we would have a more complex mapping to a time-indexed person role and corresponding subsenses that refer to the relevant properties:

```
63. :play a lemon:Word ;
       lexinfo:partOfSpeech lexinfo:verb ;
       lemon:canonicalForm [ lemon:writtenRep "play"@en ] ;

       lemon:synBehavior     [ rdf:type lexinfo:IntransitivePPFrame ;
                               lexinfo:subject            :play_arg1;
                               lexinfo:prepositionalObject :play_arg2 ] ;

       lemon:sense           [ lemon:reference soccer:PlayerRole ;
                               lemon:isA :player_role;

                               lemon:subsense [
                               lemon:reference soccer:player ;
                               lemon:subjOfProp :player_role;
                               lemon:objOfProp  :play_arg1 ];

                               lemon:subsense [
                               lemon:reference soccer:forTeam ;
                               lemon:subjOfProp :player_role ;
                               lemon:objOfProp  :play_arg2 ] ] .


     :play_arg2 lemon:marker :for .
```

Such a modeling would allow for the correct interpretation of sentences such as George Best played for Manchester United between 1963 and 1974.

Event Verbs

Many verbs do not describe states as above but instead describe *events*. Events refer to something that happens in time and has a culmination point that induces a change of state. An example of an event from the soccer domain would be a goal, which is the event corresponding to the verb to score. In RDF a particular goal may be modeled as follows:

```
64. :goal1001 a soccer:Goal ;
       soccer:byPlayer soccer:GeorgeBest ;
       soccer:forTeam  soccer:ManchesterUnited ;
       soccer:inMatch  soccer:match47 ;
       soccer:atMinute "23"^^xsd:int .
```

The above represents a frame or template consisting of three properties that have the same subject. Since in OWL there is no explicit way to refer to such frames, we need appropriate machinery to model such frames in *lemon*. For this, we assume that there is an overall sense, in this case referring to the class `Goal`, and three subsenses, each corresponding to one of the above properties, i.e., `byPlayer`, `forTeam`, `inMatch` and `atMinute`. The corresponding *lemon* entry for the verb to score would thus look as follows:

65.
```
:score a lemon:Word ;
    lemon:canonicalForm [ lemon:writtenRep "score"@en ] ;

    lemon:synBehavior   [ a lexinfo:IntransitivePPFrame ;
            lexinfo:subject            :score_subject  ;
            lexinfo:prepositionalObject :score_inObject ;
            lexinfo:prepositionalObject :score_afterObject ;
            lexinfo:prepositionalObject :score_forObject ] ;

    lemon:sense [ lemon:reference soccer:Goal ;
                lemon:isA :goal ;

                    lemon:subsense [
                    lemon:reference soccer:byPlayer ;
                    lemon:subjOfProp :goal ;
                    lemon:objOfProp  :score_subject ];

                    lemon:subsense [
                    lemon:reference soccer:inMatch ;
                    lemon:subjOfProp :goal ;
                    lemon:objOfProp  :score_inObject ];

                    lemon:subsense [
                    lemon:reference soccer:atMinute ;
                    lemon:subjOfProp :goal ;
                    lemon:objOfProp  :score_afterObject ];

                    lemon:subsense [
                    lemon:reference soccer:forTeam ;
                    lemon:subjOfProp :goal ;
                    lemon:objOfProp  :score_forObject ] ].

    :score_inObject    lemon:marker :in ;
                       lemon:optional "true"^^xsd:boolean .
    :score_afterObject lemon:marker :after ;
                       lemon:optional "true"^^xsd:boolean .
    :score_forTeam     lemon:marker :for ;
                       lemon:optional "true"^^xsd:boolean .
```

Note that one of the semantic arguments, `:goal`, is unbound in the sense that it does not occur in the syntactic frame; it is interpreted as referring to the event itself. Furthermore note that all the prepositional objects are marked as optional, which means that they may be omitted in realizations of the event. So a sentence like George Best scored a goal would be translated into

$\exists g \, (\mathrm{Goal}(g) \wedge \mathrm{byPlayer}(g, \mathrm{GeorgeBest}))$. When expressing this in RDF, one possibility is to introduce a constant to represent the existentially quantified variable g, as we did above using :goal1001.

Consequence Verbs

Consequence verbs are verbs that do not directly refer to an event but rather the consequent state of such an event. In the general case they thus cannot be directly linked to an event in the ontology to express their semantics. Take the example of the phrase was born in when expressing that someone was born in a specific place, which in the ontology might be modeled by a binary property birthPlace. The lemma of this participle is the verb to bear, for which we would specify a lexical entry, specifying born as a specific verb form. However, the meaning of the lemma to bear is certainly not the binary property birthPlace. One way of addressing this is to specify the meaning of bear as referring to a class representing the birth as an event, as in the following entry:

```
66. :bear a lemon:Word ;
      lemon:canonicalForm [ lemon:writtenRep "bear"@en ] ;

    lemon:synBehavior    [ a lexinfo:IntransitivePPFrame ;
                           lexinfo:subject             :bear_arg1 ;
                           lexinfo:directObject        :bear_arg2 ;
                           lexinfo:prepositionalObject :bear_arg3 ] ;

    lemon:sense          [ lemon:reference onto:Birth ;
                           lemon:isA :birth ;

                           lemon:subsense [
                           lemon:reference onto:mother ;
                           lemon:subjOfProp :birth ;
                           lemon:objOfProp  :bear_arg1 ];

                           lemon:subsense [
                           lemon:reference onto:child ;
                           lemon:subjOfProp :birth ;
                           lemon:objOfProp  :bear_arg2 ];

                           lemon:subsense [
                           lemon:reference onto:birthPlace ;
                           lemon:subjOfProp :birth ;
                           lemon:objOfProp  :bear_arg3 ] ] .

    :bear_arg3 lemon:marker :in .
```

4.3.4 ADJECTIVES

There have been many attempts to distinguish adjectives based on their qualities [Frawley, 1992], their implications [Abdullah and Frost, 2005] or their ontological interpretation [Raskin and Nirenburg, 1995]. Here we follow the taxonomy of adjectives proposed by Bouillon and Viegas [1999], distinguishing intersective, scalar, property-modifying, and relational adjectives.

- An adjective is *intersective* if, when modifying a noun, the semantics of the adjective-noun compound is the semantics of the adjective intersected with the semantics of the noun. For example, a dead zombie is both dead and a zombie. Such adjectives are sometimes also called *absolute*.

- An adjective is *scalar* if, when modifying a noun, the semantics of the adjective is dependent on the noun, but the semantics of the adjective-noun-compound is subsumed by the meaning of the noun. For example, an excellent striker is a striker but is not, per se, excellent (he may not be an excellent father, for example). Such adjectives are also called *relative* or *subsective*.

- *Property-modifying adjectives* are adjectives where the meaning of the semantics of the adjective-noun-compound is not necessarily subsumed by the semantics of the adjective or the noun. For example, a former player is neither a player nor former per se. They may also be referred to as *privative*, *non-intersective* or as *operators*. The use of the term *operator* is due to the understanding that such adjectives represent a relationship between two qualia (i.e., intersective classes) [Bouillon and Viegas, 1999].

- *Relational adjectives* are adjectives that describe a relation between two entities, such as made of and like. They require a second argument realized through a prepositional phrase or a genitive, dative or other phrase. Frequently they cannot be used attributively (Peter is like Cantona is fine, but the like Peter is not).

There is one important remark to be made here. The main difference between intersective and the other classes of adjectives is whether the meaning of the adjective depends on the noun it combines with or not. If it does, researchers from the *generative lexicon* tradition [Pustejovsky, 1991] talk about *co-composition*. In our view, there are very few examples of clearly intersective adjectives. Many adjectives that are typically considered as intersective in the literature are clearly not. Take the adjective red. A discrete category *red* does not exist universally. Assuming that *red* actually represents a continuous distribution over the color space or even a prototype, then it is quite obvious that the noun with which red combines will shift this distribution, for example the color distribution of red hair is going to be different from that of a red car.

In the following we discuss how the different classes of adjectives introduced above can be modeled in *lemon*.

Intersective Adjectives

Consider the example dead with the following lexical entry:

```
67. :dead a lemon:Word ;
       lexinfo:partOfSpeech lexinfo:adjective ;
       lemon:canonicalForm [ lemon:writtenRep "dead"@en ] ;

       lemon:synBehavior    [ a lexinfo:AdjectivePredicateFrame ;
                              lexinfo:copulativeSubject :dead_arg ] ;

       lemon:sense          [ lemon:reference onto:Dead ;
                              lemon:isA :dead_arg ].
```

In this case the modeling is similar to the one for class nouns in the sense that the semantics is expressed by a single class, here the class Dead of dead creatures. We use the
AdjectivePredicateFrame, which is equivalent to the intersection of a predicative frame (capturing predicative usages as in the zombie is dead) and an attributive frame (capturing attributive
usages as in the dead zombie), in order to indicate that the adjective has both attributive and predicative usage. The concept Dead is either defined in the domain ontology or at the lexicon-ontology
interface, possibly defined as Dead $\equiv \exists$ dateOfDeath.$\top$.

Scalar Adjectives

There are many different ways to model the semantics of scalar adjectives such as excellent (like in
excellent striker), depending on the ontology in question:

- The ontology could directly include a class ExcellentStriker.

- The ontology might have a property soccerPlayingSkills with different values such as
  average, good, excellent, top, etc.

- The ontology might decide to model the excellence of players by saying that the average
  number of goals scored per game needs to be higher than 0.5 for a striker to be excellent.

- The ontology might decide that excellent players are those whose market worth is in the top
  5% of professional players.

For the first three cases the modeling quickly reduces to a standard intersective adjective,
where all except the first one require the introduction of a class with appropriate axioms. The
final case is the most challenging one, as this predicate is clearly non-monotonic: If we acquire
knowledge about more players, then it is possible that some other players are no longer in the
top 5% and hence are no longer deemed excellent. OWL 2 DL allows for the modeling of only
monotonic, open-world logic and as such it is not possible to correctly capture the semantics of
this predicate. The solution to this is to extend the semantics of the ontology to capture predicates
that can be used in the interpretation system. This is done by a small auxiliary vocabulary, called

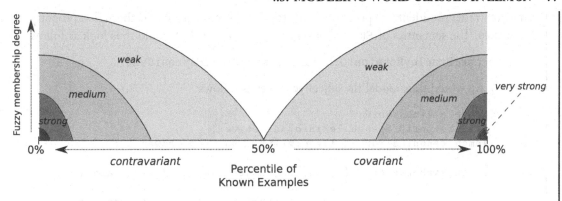

Figure 4.4: The degrees of membership to fuzzy classes of scalar adjectives.

lemonOILS, the *lemon Ontology for the Interpretation of Lexical Semantics*. In this case we can model excellent as referring to a class of `Excellent` things, without specifying in OWL2 DL how we assert that something is excellent. Instead we add annotations that indicate the scalar assertion. For example:

```
68. @prefix oils: <http://www.lemon-model.net/oils#> .

    :excellent rdfs:subClassOf  oils:CovariantScalar ;
               oils:boundTo      onto:marketWorth ;
               oils:degree       oils:strong .
```

This states that the semantics of the adjective excellent is defined with respect to the property `marketWorth` the value of which needs to be `strong` for a player to count as excellent. Further, the extent to which a player is excellent is proportional (or *covariant*) to his or her market worth in the sense that as the market worth increases, so does the excellence of the player. The values for degrees are shown in Figure 4.4 (based on Raskin and Nirenburg [1995]), in comparison to the likelihood that the instance would be judged to belong to the class in relation to what percentile of known examples it belongs to. Note that scalar adjectives may be *covariant*, *contravariant* or *central*, the latter meaning that the fuzzy membership is evaluated by way of its closeness or distance to some prototypical member.

Property-Modifying Adjectives

Property-modifying adjectives are characterized by the fact that the semantics of the adjective-noun compound is not generally subsumed by the semantics of the noun. Consider the case of former with the stereotypical frame *X* is a former *Y* or *X* is the former *Y*. Obviously a former president is not a president anymore, so that the set of former presidents is clearly not subsumed by the set of (current) presidents. A principled way to model such adjectives is through a property, e.g., heldRole. The semantics of Stanley Rous is a former FIFA president would thus look as follows:

69. `soccer:StanleyRous onto:heldRole soccer:FIFApresident .`

In *lemon* we would thus model the adjective former as follows:

```
70. :former a lemon:Word;
      lexinfo:partOfSpeech lexinfo:adjective ;
      lemon:canonicalForm [ lemon:writtenRep "former"@en ] ;

      lemon:synBehavior    [ a lexinfo:AdjectiveAttributiveFrame ;
                             lexinfo:copulativeSubject :former_arg1 ;
                             lexinfo:attributiveArg     :former_arg2 ;

      lemon:sense          [ lemon:reference onto:heldRole ;
                             lemon:subjOfProp :former_arg1 ;
                             lemon:objOfProp  :former_arg2 ] .
```

While property-modifying adjectives can be used predicatively, in general they cannot be used attributively. In cases where this is possible, e.g., for fake as in this gun is fake and a fake gun, we have to introduce a class that existentially quantifies over that entity which the given entity is a forgery of. If the property that the adjective fake is associated to is forgeryOf, then the semantics of the attributive usage of fake can be represented by a class Fake defined as follows:

71. $Fake \equiv \exists forgeryOf.Thing$

Relational Adjectives

Relational adjectives behave similarly to relational nouns in the sense that they express a relation between two individuals. The adjective made of, for example, can be modeled in *lemon* as follows:

```
72. :made a lemon:Word ;
      lexinfo:partOfSpeech lexinfo:adjective ;
      lemon:canonicalform [ lemon:writtenRep "made"@en ] ;

      lemon:synBehaviour  [ a lexinfo:AdjectivePPFrame ;
                            lexinfo:copulativeSubject    :made_arg1 ;
                            lexinfo:prepositionalObject :made_arg2 ];

      lemon:sense         [ lemon:reference onto:material ;
                            lemon:subjOfProp :made_arg1 ;
                            lemon:objOfProp  :made_arg2 ] .

    :made_arg2 lemon:marker :of .
```

In contrast to relational nouns (such as capital), where we specified a copulative argument that could be both subject and object of a copulative constructions (as in Berlin is the capital of

Germany and The capital of Germany is Berlin), we use a *copulative subject*, as the adjective itself can only be the object of the sentence (as in This toy is made of wood, but not Made of wood is this toy). The second argument is a *prepositional object* as the object is marked with the preposition of.

4.3.5   ADVERBS

Adverbs form a wide class of words and have been claimed to be a catch-all category in syntax. Adverbs can indeed modify sentences, verbs, adjectives or other adverbs. We encounter all these different cases in the following sentence:

73. Typically, only the very quickly evolving species adapt well.

In this example typically modifies the sentence, only modifies the noun phrase, very modifies the adverb quickly which in turn modifies the adjective evolving, and well modifies the verb.

Adverbs that are derived from adjectives (e.g., quickly) and modify either another adjective or a verb can be modeled analogously to adjectives in the sense of expressing either some property of the class denoted by the adjective or of the event denoted by the verb. In general, however, the modeling of adverbs requires an ontology of modality (e.g., to express the meaning of an adverb such as possible) or appropriate ontological theories of time and space to express the meaning of temporal adverbs such as often or spatial adverbs such as everywhere. The development of appropriate microtheories of time, space and modality is beyond the scope of this book.

4.4   FURTHER READING

The lexicon for our soccer ontology can be downloaded at the book website.

The modeling of the ontological semantics of closed-class words of nouns, verbs and adjectives is inspired and directly related to the modeling of these parts of speech in the Ontological Semantics framework of Nirenburg and Raskin [2004]. In general, nouns are from a computational semantics point of view usually regarded as simply denoting a class or set of individuals. We have seen that some nouns are more complex than that, including relational nouns. Theoretical issues arising with relational nouns are for instance discussed by Dekker [1993] and de Bruin and Scha [1988]. Our treatment of adjectives follows quite closely the treatment of adjectives in the framework of Ontological Semantics [Raskin and Nirenburg, 1995].

There are various papers on *lemon*. McCrae et al. [2011] and McCrae et al. [2012b] discuss aspects related to interoperability and how *lemon* can be used to model and represent linguistic resources. The paper by Cimiano et al. [2013] discusses theoretical aspects related to the role of sense objects in the lexicon-ontology interface. *lemon* was based on a precursor model called LexInfo [Cimiano et al., 2011], which included a specific ontology of parts of speech and of subcategorization frames. *lemon* has been designed so that it is agnostic to the particular ontology adopted. Since the original publication, the range of categories that LexInfo supports has been increased notably. McCrae and Cimiano [2012] and McCrae et al. [2012c] propose a collaborative methodology for the creation of *lemon* lexica.

In order to support lexicon engineers in the construction of lexical entries, *lemon* comes with a design patterns library [McCrae and Unger, to appear], which defines macros for the most common kinds of lexical entries, thereby making them shorter, more concise and easier to write and read than RDF.

CHAPTER 5

Grammar Generation

A full-fledged grammar consists of at least two parts: a domain-specific part using a vocabulary aligned to the ontology, as we saw in Chapter 3, and a domain-independent part comprising closed-class expressions such as determiners, pronouns, auxiliary verbs, conjunction and negation, possibly further extended with temporal, modal and other expressions. The latter part has to be created manually, but can be reused across domains and applications. However, as we will see in this chapter, the ontology-specific grammar can be created automatically from an ontology lexicon in *lemon* format.

5.1 FROM ONTOLOGY LEXICA TO GRAMMARS

Grammar development is an effort-intensive process. Especially with large domains it becomes hard to build, extend and maintain the corresponding grammars. Moreover, in the context of ontology-based interpretation, the creation of grammars requires particular care, as we want our syntactic and semantic representations to be aligned to the underlying ontology (see Sections 3.3 and 3.5 in Chapter 3). But most of all, creating grammars involves a high amount of redundancy. For transitive verbs, for example, we need LTAG trees that cover the active form, both in all present and past tense variants, as well as the passive form, the participle and gerund use, etc. The general structure of these trees is the same for all verbs. It is thus an obvious thought that the specific trees for a particular verb could and should be generated from some more general pattern.

Ontology lexica as introduced in Chapter 4 can considerably help as the basis for the generation of grammars. They provide a compact declarative, theory-neutral representation of syntactic and semantic aspects of lexical items and thus abstract from particular instantiations of different word forms in a specific grammar formalism. Moreover, they specify the meaning of lexical entries with respect to an ontology and therefore facilitate the generation of semantic representations that are aligned to the structure and vocabulary of that ontology.

In the following we will illustrate how an ontology lexicon can be used as a source for automatically generating LTAG/DUDES grammars. First note that a *lemon* lexicon indeed contains all linguistic information needed for constructing LTAG trees and DUDES: morphological information about the different forms of a lexical item, such as present, past and participle forms for verbs, syntactic information about the number and kind of arguments that the lexical item requires, semantic information about the reference of the item with respect to the underlying ontology as well as information about how the semantic arguments correspond to the syntactic arguments. Consider the following *lemon* entry as an example, specifying a verbalization of the property playsFor:

74. ```
:play a lemon:Word ;
    lexinfo:partOfSpeech lexinfo:verb ;

    lemon:canonicalForm [lemon:writtenRep "play"@en] ;
    lemon:otherForm   [lemon:writtenRep "played"@en ;
                          lexinfo:tense lexinfo:past] ;

    lemon:synBehavior   [a lexinfo:IntransitivePPFrame ;
                          lexinfo:subject   :x ;
                          lexinfo:prepositionalObject :y] ;

    lemon:sense   [lemon:reference soccer:playsFor ;
                          lemon:subjOfProp :x ;
                          lemon:objOfProp :y]] .

:play_arg2 lemon:marker :for .
```

This entry specifies the syntactic and morphological information that is required to generate corresponding LTAG trees, as well as the semantic information required for constructing a DUDES.

Since the part of speech is verb, we know that the overall structure of the LTAG trees should be that of a sentence tree. Moreover, the syntactic behavior specifies to play for as an intransitive verb with an accompanying prepositional phrase; the tree should thus be composed of a verb phrase comprising the verb and a PP with the preposition for, as well as a subject DP. The tree would thus look as follows:

75.

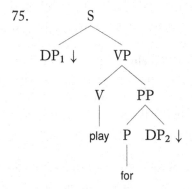

We need similar trees for the third person singular form plays and the past form played, as well as an adjoining tree for the gerundive form playing.

**Exercise 5.1**   Specify the NP adjunction tree for the gerund playing that is needed to capture phrases like all strikers playing for Manchester United.
```

Semantically, play for refers to the two-place predicate `soccer:playsFor`, the first argument of which is contributed by the syntactic subject and the second argument of which is contributed by the prepositional object, captured in the following semantic representation:

76.
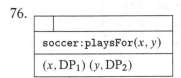

Exercise 5.2   Construct a similar DUDES that corresponds to the gerund tree from Exercise 5.1.

The general approach to constructing syntactic and semantic representation from lexicon entries is the following: Based on the part of speech and the syntactic behavior, extract all relevant information from the lexical entry, such as different word forms, syntactic and semantic arguments as well as their correspondence, and use this information to fill corresponding LTAG tree and DUDES templates. In the following we demonstrate this strategy with respect to the word classes described in Chapter 4.

5.2   GENERATING NOUN ENTRIES

Proper nouns are fairly simple. They have only one morphological form and do not require any arguments. The general form of a *lemon* entry for proper nouns is given in 77a. The template for proper nouns thus specifies a simple DP tree together with a simple DUDES for individuals, as shown in 77b. Note that only the written representation and the URI—marked in bold face—are specific to the example; the rest will be the same for every proper noun entry. Accordingly, the bold-faced parts of the LTAG tree and DUDES are specific instantiations, while the rest represents the general part of the template for proper nouns.

77.   (a)   `:entry a lemon:LexicalEntry ;`
            `lexinfo:partOfSpeech lexinfo:properNoun ;`

            `lemon:canonicalForm [ lemon:writtenRep ''Uruguay"@en ];`
            `lemon:sense          [ lemon:reference soccer:Uruguay ] ] .`

    (b)   DP
            |
            Uruguay

$$\begin{array}{|l|l|}\hline x & x \\ \hline x = \mathbf{soccer{:}Uruguay} \\ \hline \\ \hline \end{array}$$

Class nouns, such as goal and team, have a *lemon* entry as given in 78a. Again, the bold-faced parts are specific to the example, while the rest is general. They correspond to an NP tree together with a semantic representation containing a unary predicate. But now it does not suffice to construct one grammar entry, because we have two forms—a singular form and a plural form. In order to capture all uses of English class NPs, we need three grammar entries: a singular and a plural NP, given in 78b, as well as a determiner-less plural DP for the generic use, as in a soccer league without teams, given in 78c. The semantic representations for these differ only in that the DP denotation introduces the referent marker x into the DRS universe, while the NP denotation does not. In the latter case, the marker will be introduced by the determiner with which the NP is combined.

78. (a) `:entry a lemon:LexicalEntry ;`
`        lexinfo:partOfSpeech lexinfo:noun ;`

`        lemon:canonicalForm [ lemon:writtenRep ''team"@en ;`
`                              lexinfo:number lexinfo:singular ];`
`        lemon:otherForm     [ lemon:writtenRep ''teams@en ;`
`                              lexinfo:number lexinfo:plural ];`

`        lemon:synBehavior   [ a lexinfo:NounPredicateFrame;`
`                              lexinfo:copulativeArg :x ];`

`        lemon:sense         [ lemon:reference soccer:Team ;`
`                              lemon:isA :x ] ] .`

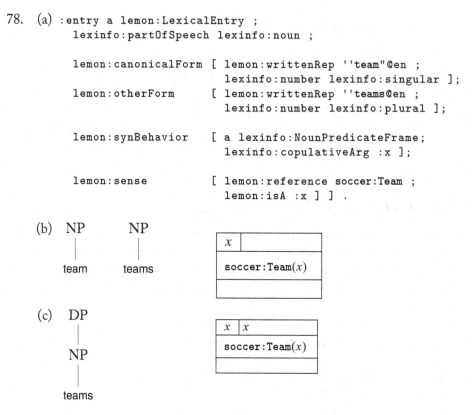

Relational nouns such as capacity differ from class nouns in their syntactic behavior and sense. As exemplified in 79a, they subcategorize for an argument which can usually be expressed either as a prepositional object as in the capacity of the stadium, or as a possessive as in the stadium's capacity. Syntactically, relational nouns therefore constitute NP trees (or a DP tree in the generic case) with a substitution node for the argument. The singular trees for both the prepositional and the possessive realization, together with their meaning, are given in 79b. The plural trees as well as corresponding generic DP trees are analogous. Their meaning is represented as a binary predicate corresponding to the ontology property.

79. (a) `:entry a lemon:LexicalEntry ;`
            `lexinfo:partOfSpeech lexinfo:noun ;`

```
lemon:canonicalForm  [ lemon:writtenRep ''capacity"@en ;
                       lexinfo:number lexinfo:singular ];

lemon:synBehavior    [ a lexinfo:NounPossessiveFrame;
                       lexinfo:copulativeArg      :y ;
                       lexinfo:possessiveAdjunct :x ];

lemon:sense          [ lemon:reference soccer:capacity ;
                       lemon:subjOfProp :x ;
                       lemon:objOfProp  :y ] ] .
```

(b)

Note that the DUDES contains only one selection pair, as the LTAG tree contains only one substitution node. The copulative argument y is not selected by the noun, but only occurs higher in the tree in constructions like y is the capacity of the stadium. Semantically such a construction will come out right, as y is the main variable. We will see an example of such a meaning composition in Chapter 6.

5.3   GENERATING VERB ENTRIES

The grammar entries for verbs are generated on the basis of the number and kind of their syntactic arguments, independent of whether the verb denotes a state or event. We will look at the two most important classes of verbs: intransitive verbs, with or without prepositional objects, and transitive verbs, again with or without prepositional objects.

Intransitive verbs require only a subject. An example is to win, with a lexical entry as given in 80a. In LTAG terms, intransitive verbs are represented as trees like the one given in 80b. In the context of our soccer ontology the lexical sense specifies the relation winner as reference of the verb, with the syntactic subject as the first argument and an unbound second argument. In the DUDES, the first argument occurs in the selection pair, as it will be provided by the subject DP meaning, while the second argument occurs in the discourse universe and thus is interpreted as existentially quantified. The sentence y wins therefore means that there is some x (a game or a tournament) that y is the winner of.

80. (a) `:win a lemon:LexicalEntry ;`
         `lexinfo:partOfSpeech lexinfo:verb ;`

         `lemon:canonicalForm [ lemon:writtenRep ''win"@en ];`

         `lemon:synBehavior    [ a lexinfo:IntransitiveFrame;`
                              `lexinfo:subject :y ];`

         `lemon:sense          [ lemon:reference onto:winner ;`
                              `lemon:subjOfProp :x ;`
                              `lemon:objOfProp  :y ] .`

(b)

In addition, the grammar generation process should construct analogous entries for other forms, such as the third person singular form wins and the past form won. For now we can assume that the semantic representation is the same; in Chapter 8 we will then have a closer look at the treatment of temporal aspects.

Another common case is the one of intransitive verbs that refer to a class in the ontology, as in the lexical entry in 81a (leaving out all forms other than the canonical form). The tree representation is the same as above, as nothing in the syntactic behavior has changed, only the meaning representation slightly differs.

81. (a) `:surf a lemon:LexicalEntry ;`
         `lexinfo:partOfSpeech lexinfo:verb ;`

         `lemon:canonicalForm [ lemon:writtenRep ''surf"@en ];`

         `lemon:synBehavior    [ a lexinfo:IntransitiveFrame;`
                              `lexinfo:subject :x ];`

         `lemon:sense          [ lemon:reference onto:Surfer ;`
                              `lemon:isA :x ] ] .`

(b)

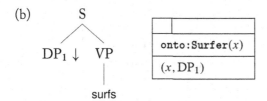

We have already provided an example of an intransitive verb with a prepositional object (see 74 and 75) at the beginning of the chapter.

Transitive verbs subcategorize for a subject as well as a direct object. An example is to respect, with a lexical entry as given in 82a (glossing over other forms, such as respects, respected, and respecting), which assumes that our soccer ontology contains an object property respect that relates persons to each other, in particular players, referees and fans. The LTAG tree for the present form, given in 82b, is not surprising; neither is the DUDES. The tree and meaning representations for the past form are the same.

82. (a)
```
:respect a lemon:LexicalEntry ;
    lexinfo:partOfSpeech lexinfo:verb ;

    lemon:canonicalForm [ lemon:writtenRep ''respect"@en ] ;

    lemon:synBehavior    [ a lexinfo:TransitiveFrame;
                           lexinfo:subject       :x ;
                           lexinfo:directObject :y ];

    lemon:sense          [ lemon:reference soccer:respect ;
                           lemon:subjOfProp :x ;
                           lemon:objOfProp  :y ] ] .
```

(b)

```
            S
          /   \
     DP₁ ↓     VP
              /  \
             V    DP₂ ↓
             |
          respects
```

$$soccer:respect(x, y)$$
$$(x, DP_1)\ (y, DP_2)$$

But this does not suffice. We also need to construct grammar entries that capture the different syntactic frames or constructions in which transitive verbs occur. One of them is the passive construction, as exemplified in 83. Note that the object DP now occurs in subject position and the subject DP is a prepositional argument, while the meaning representation does not change.

83.

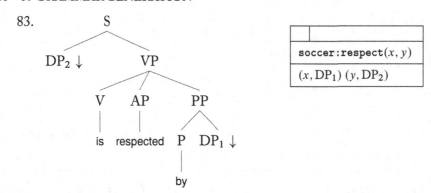

Another construction is NP modifiers, as in all players respecting the referee and a referee respected by all players. Since respecting the referee and respected by all players are NP modifiers, i.e., optional attachments to an NP, the LTAG trees are NP adjunction trees, as specified in 84a and 84b. The semantic representation is as before, with the only exception that only one argument is specified in the selection pairs, while the other argument will be provided by the NP to which the tree is adjoined.

84.   (a)

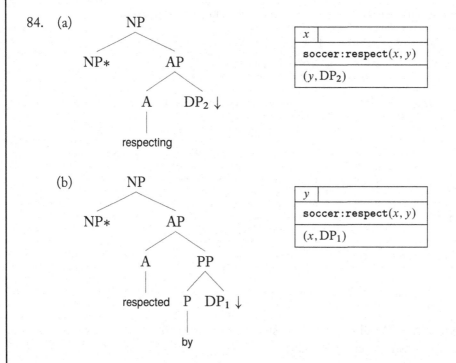

Very similar are relative clause constructions, for which grammar entries are shown in 85a and 85b.

85. (a)

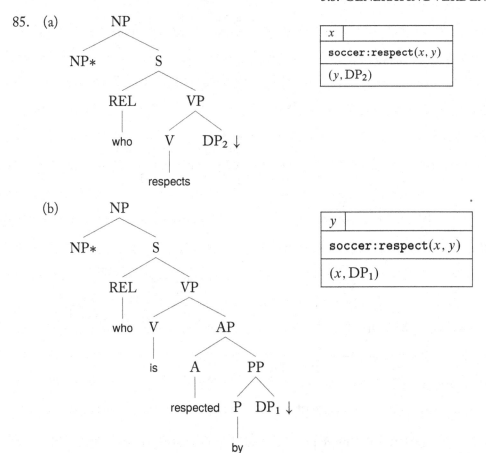

x	
`soccer:respect`(x, y)	
(y, DP_2)	

(b)

y	
`soccer:respect`(x, y)	
(x, DP_1)	

Finally, transitive verbs can take prepositional objects; examples are the verbs lead to, as in Ronaldo led his team to its first victory, and win against, as in Barcelona won yesterday's match against Madrid. The lexical entry for win against is given in 86a, again leaving out most forms. How exactly the sense is composed depends on the kind of state or event the verb denotes. Here it simply consists of two object properties, one between what was won and the winner, and the other between what was won and the loser. The grammar entry thus specifies a tree with three DP substitution nodes, and a semantic representation involving two predicates, winner and loser, the arguments of which are contributed by the meanings of that DPs, as specified in 86b.

86. (a) :win_against a lemon:LexicalEntry ;
         lexinfo:partOfSpeech lexinfo:verb ;

         lemon:canonicalForm [lemon:writtenRep ''win"@en] ;

         lemon:synBehavior   [rdf:type lexinfo:TransitivePPFrame;
                                lexinfo:subject   :x ;

```
                                    lexinfo:directObject        :z ;
                                    lexinfo:prepositionalObject :y ];

        lemon:sense           [ lemon:subsense [
                                lemon:reference soccer:winner ;
                                lemon:subjOfProp :z ;
                                lemon:objOfProp  :x ] ;

                                lemon:subsense [
                                lemon:reference soccer:loser ;
                                lemon:subjOfProp :z ;
                                lemon:objOfProp  :y ] ] .

        :y lemon:marker :against .
```

(b)

Verbs with two, three or more prepositional objects are treated analogously. Their lexical entries would enumerate more prepositional objects (with the syntactic frame staying the same, i.e., `IntransitivePPFrame` or `TransitivePPFrame`) and probably more subsenses, and the corresponding grammar entries would accordingly comprise more PPs and more selection pairs.

5.4 GENERATING ADJECTIVE ENTRIES

Without diving into all different adjective frames, we just look at a simple example, the adjective suspended, which can be used both attributively, as in all suspended players, and predicatively, as in that player is suspended. It has a simple intersective meaning, modeled in our ontology through a datatype property suspended mapping players to Boolean values. The lexical entry would then look as in 87a. It specifies a syntactic frame that subsumes both the attributive and predicative usage. It therefore lists both an *attributive argument* for the attributive usage and a *copulative subject* for the predicative usage; they are the same as they both denote the suspended player. In the constructed grammar entries, we want to likewise capture both the attributive and the predicative use and therefore generate the trees in 87b and 87c. The former is a simple noun modifier, while the latter gives rise to a sentence representation; nevertheless, their semantic representations are the same.

87. (a)

```
:suspended a lemon:LexicalEntry ;
    lexinfo:partOfSpeech lexinfo:adjective ;

    lemon:canonicalForm [ lemon:writtenRep ''suspended''@en ];

    lemon:synBehavior   [ a lexinfo:AdjectivePredicateFrame;
                          lexinfo:attributiveArg    :x ;
                          lexinfo:copulativeSubject :x ];

    lemon:sense         [ lemon:reference soccer:suspended ;
                          lemon:subjOfProp :x ;
                          lemon:objOfProp  "true"^^xsd:boolean ]].
```

(b)

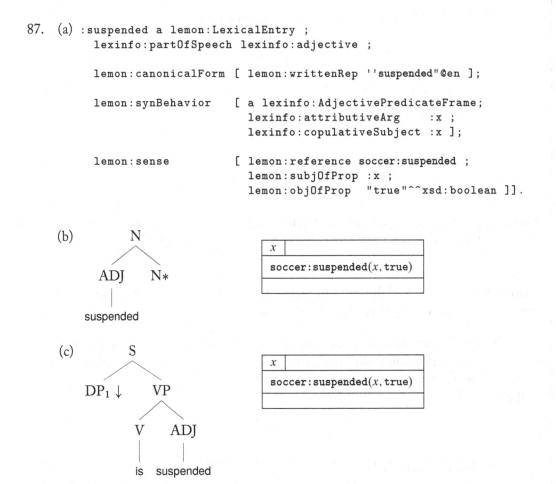

(c)

In addition, an entry as in 87a would give rise to trees like 87c but with are, was and were instead of is.

Usually we also want to specify the comparative and superlative form in the lexicon, although this is not applicable in the case of suspended as it is not a scalar adjective (either you are suspended or not). For the comparative form of the adjective tall, for example, we want to generate a grammar entry like the one in 88. If tall is bound to a datatype property `height` in our ontology, the sentence x is taller than y means that the height of x is greater than the height of y. Note that in order to know that it needs to be greater and not less, as would be the case of x is smaller than y, the lexicon needs to specify whether the adjective is covariant (like tall) or contravariant (like small); recall the discussion on scalar adjectives in Chapter 4.

88.

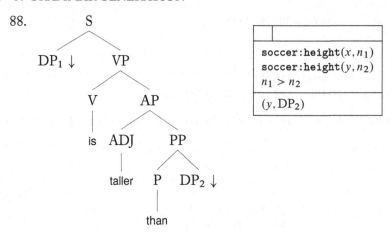

Exercise 5.3 Construct an additional noun-modifying AP tree with an appropriate semantic representation, that captures adjective uses like players taller than Jan Koller.

Exercise 5.4 What would the semantic representation of taller than need to look like in order to capture the comparative construction taller than 1.90?

The superlative form (tallest) requires another grammar entry, as given in 89a. The DUDES makes use of a duplex condition (see Section 3.7) that expresses that the height of the main referent of the NP meaning needs to be maximal with respect to all other heights. This corresponds to the first-order logical formula in 89b.

89. (a)

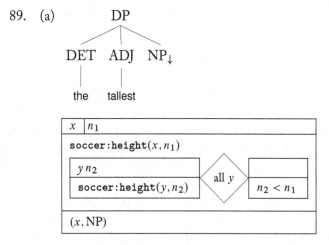

(b) $\exists n_1 (\texttt{height}(x, n_1) \wedge \forall y, n_2 (\texttt{height}(y, n_2) \rightarrow n_2 < n_1))$

5.5   IMPLEMENTATION

We have seen that in general we require a large amount of different grammar entries, capturing all forms and syntactic behaviors of the given lexical items. This is the main reason why creating grammars by hand is a very laborious and also tedious work, and why it is desirable to generate grammars automatically from a much denser lexicon representation. We sketched an approach that uses all relevant information contained in a lexical entry in order to instantiate a template that specifies the general form of syntactic and semantic representations corresponding to that particular kind of entry. A corresponding algorithm can be sketched as follows:

For each entry e in the lexicon:

1. Get the part of speech of e.

2. Based on the part of speech, get all relevant word forms provided by e.
   For nouns this comprises the singular and plural form, for verbs the present and past tense forms as well as participle and gerund forms, and for adjectives the positive, comparative and superlative forms.

3. Get all senses of e, including the reference and semantic arguments.

4. Get all syntactic behaviors. Then for each syntactic behavior s:

   (a) Get the involved syntactic arguments together with argument-specific information, such as optionality and markers.

   (b) Find a template for s and instantiate it using the word forms, the syntactic arguments and the senses. These templates specify the general form of the LTAG trees relevant for s and the corresponding DUDES, i.e., they look like the representations we have shown throughout the chapter, containing placeholders instead of the bold-faced parts.

   (c) If no template for s is found, use a general template for the part of speech as fallback.

The only part of the above algorithm that is language-specific is the linguistic representations specified in the templates. Thus, when porting the grammar generation method to a new language, one mainly needs to provide templates for that language. Note that while the syntactic structures usually differ between languages, the semantic representations are always shared in our case, due to the use of an ontology as normalizing vocabulary.

A pointer to an implementation of a mapping from *lemon* lexica to LTAG/DUDES grammars, relying on the RDF query language SPARQL[1] for extracting information from the lexicon and on Mustache[2] as templating language, can be found on the book website.

[1] http://www.w3.org/TR/sparql11-overview/
[2] http://mustache.github.io/

5.6   FURTHER READING

With the rise of NLP also came an increasing interest in wide-coverage grammars. In the context of TAG this has led to ongoing efforts in developing comprehensive TAG grammars, for instance for French [Abeillé et al., 1999], English [XTAG Research Group, 2001], and Korean [Han et al., 2000]. Because the development of such grammars involves a lot of effort and redundancy, methodologies have been developed for compiling trees from so-called metagrammars, i.e., descriptions of trees based on generalizations of linguistic structures and tree structure sharing. A quite mature framework for metagrammar compilation is XMG[3] [Crabbé et al., 2013], which has been used, e.g., for creating a German TAG grammar [Kallmeyer et al., 2008].

Since *lemon* lexica are declarative and theory-neutral, they can serve as a basis for the generation of grammars also using other target formalisms. While we have not discussed this in more detail in this chapter, we have also implemented a grammar generation component that generates Grammatical Framework [Ranta, 2011] grammars from lemon lexica (see `http://lemon-model.net/lemon2gf.html`).

---

[3]`http://wiki.loria.fr/wiki/XMG/Documentation`

CHAPTER 6

Putting Everything Together

In this chapter we will demonstrate how everything we have shown so far works together in order to get from a domain conceptualization and a corresponding lexicon to domain-specific semantic representations of utterances.

Using an example, we will walk through the whole process of conceptualization, lexicon creation and semantic interpretation. The goal is to give you a flavor of the big picture and provide as comprehensive an overview as possible of what is involved in the ontology-based interpretation of natural language. Then we will touch upon some interesting challenges that one encounters in this enterprise.

6.1 FROM CONCEPTUALIZATIONS TO MEANING REPRESENTATIONS

Consider the following example:

90. Chelsea won because of a goal by Drogba in the third minute.

Let us look at how the conceptualization of this sentence can be captured in an ontology, what lexical entries are required for verbalizing these entries, and how the resulting grammar entries combine to yield a meaning representation aligned to the ontology.

Using the soccer ontology we have developed in Chapter 2, we assume a class of matches, a class of persons, in our case mainly soccer players, referees and coaches, and a general class of soccer events that comprises goals and all kinds of soccer actions, such as free kicks, shots on goals, passes, yellow cards, and so on. Soccer actions are connected to a person by means of the property byPlayer and to a soccer event by means of leadsTo, e.g., a foul can lead to a yellow or red card, and a shot on the goal can lead to a goal. Soccer events are related to the match they are part of via the property inMatch, and to the minute of the match at which they occur via the datatype property atMinute. The match itself is related to a winning and a losing team. This is depicted in Figure 6.1.

With respect to this conceptualization, the sentence in 90 expresses that there was a soccer action by player Drogba at minute 3 that led to a goal and caused Chelsea to be winner. Ignoring the causal relation for now, an intended state of affairs capturing such a situation is described by the following RDF triples:

91. :x rdf:type soccer:Goal .
    :y rdf:type soccer:Match .

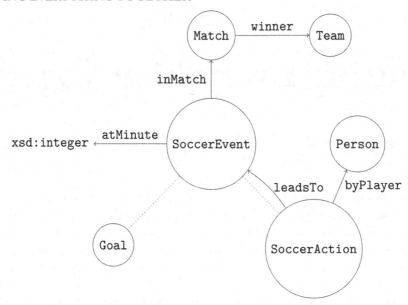

Figure 6.1: Part of the soccer ontology relevant for the sentence Chelsea won because of a goal by Drogba in the third minute.

```
:z rdf:type soccer:SoccerAction .

:z soccer:byPlayer soccer:DidierDrogba .
:z soccer:leadsTo :x .
:x soccer:atMinute "3"^^xsd:int .
:x soccer:inMatch :y .
:y soccer:winner soccer:ChelseaFC .
```

In order to be able to correctly interpret a sentence like 90, we need corresponding grammar entries. First of all, let us separate domain-independent and domain-specific expressions occurring in that sentence. The domain-independent expressions have a fixed grammar entry in the closed-class part of our grammar, while grammar entries for the domain-specific expressions will be automatically generated from lexical entries.

Obviously, the names Drogba and Chelsea are domain-specific, while the determiner a is domain-independent. The grammar entry for a is given in 92. Syntactically, it is of category DET and subcategorizes for a noun phrase; semantically, its only role is to introduce an existentially quantified discourse referent that will be unified with the main variable of the NP meaning.

92.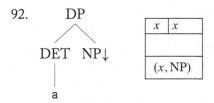

For the named individuals Drogba and Chelsea, we use the following lexical entries, according to *lemon*'s modeling of proper nouns described in Section 4.3.1 of Chapter 4:

93. `:Drogba a lemon:LexicalEntry ;`
```
     lexinfo:partOfSpeech   lexinfo:properNoun ;
     lemon:canonicalForm [ lemon:writtenRep "Drogba"@en ];
     lemon:sense         [ lemon:reference soccer:DidierDrogba ].
```

```
    :Chelsea a lemon:LexicalEntry ;
     lexinfo:partOfSpeech   lexinfo:properNoun ;
     lemon:canonicalForm [ lemon:writtenRep "Chelsea"@en ];
     lemon:sense         [ lemon:reference soccer:ChelseaFC ].
```

From these entries, the grammar generation method will straightforwardly construct corresponding grammar entries, as in 77b on page 83.

The verb won is clearly also domain-specific. It refers to the ontological property `winner`. Syntactically, we would be inclined to say that it is a transitive verb, relating the winner to what was won. However, in the sentence 90, it is used intransitively; what was won is not explicitly mentioned but remains implicit. When modeling to win in the lexicon, we therefore specify two syntactic behaviors: a transitive one and an intransitive one. The entry would then look as follows:

94. `:win a lemon:Word ;`
```
     lexinfo:partOfSpeech lexinfo:verb ;
     lemon:canonicalForm [ lemon:writtenRep "win"@en ];

     lemon:synBehavior    [ a lexinfo:IntransitiveFrame ;
                            lexinfo:subject :win_arg1 ] ,
                          [ a lexinfo:TransitiveFrame ;
                            lexinfo:subject      :win_arg1 ;
                            lexinfo:directObject :win_arg2 ] ;

     lemon:sense          [ lemon:reference soccer:winner ;
                            lemon:subjOfProp :win_arg2 ;
                            lemon:objOfProp  :win_arg1 ] .
```

Given this lexical entry, the grammar generation method should generate two grammar entries, one with a transitive verb tree and a corresponding semantics, in which both arguments of `winner` are syntactically realized, as in 95a, and one with an intransitive tree and a corresponding semantics, where the second argument of `winner` is existentially quantified, as in 95b. (We use the past tense form here, as this is what we need for our sentence 90.)

95.   (a)

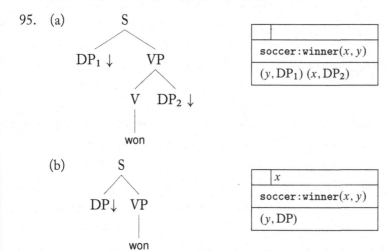

(b)

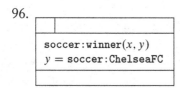

A composed representation of the meaning of Chelsea won then is the following:

96.

soccer:winner(x, y)
$y = $ soccer:ChelseaFC

Exercise 6.1   In Section 3.6 we saw a grammar entry for the verb won against. Construct a lexical entry for to win that captures all the following usages:

97.   (a) Chelsea won.

(b) Chelsea won the game.

(c) Chelsea won against Madrid.

(d) Chelsea won the game against Madrid.

How would the grammar entries that need to be generated from that lexical entry for 97c and 97d look?

Now let us move to the determiner phrase a goal by Drogba in the third minute. The noun goal is again clearly domain-specific, but what about the preposition by? If it is domain-independent, which domain-independent meaning should it have, such that its combination with the meaning of goal (arguably simply the class of goals) yields the meaning of goal by (according to the conceptualization in 6.1 a goal to which a soccer event led that was executed by a certain player)?

With the means we have at hand so far, the most straightforward solution is to assume that goal by is an expression with respect to our domain, namely the noun goal with a prepositional argument marked with by, such as in the following lexical entry:

```
97. :goal_by a lemon:LexicalEntry ;
        lexinfo:partOfSpeech lexinfo:noun ;
        lemon:canonicalForm [ lemon:writtenRep "goal"@en ];

        lemon:synBehavior     [ a lexinfo:NounPossessiveFrame ;
                                lexinfo:copulativeArg      :goal ;
                                lexinfo:possessiveAdjunct :player ];

        lemon:sense           [ lemon:subsense [
                                lemon:reference soccer:Goal ;
                                lemon:isA :goal ],

                                lemon:subsense [
                                lemon:reference soccer:leadsTo ;
                                lemon:subjOfProp :action;
                                lemon:objOfProp  :goal ],

                                lemon:subsense [
                                lemon:reference soccer:byPlayer ;
                                lemon:subjOfProp :action ;
                                lemon:objOfProp  :player ] ] .

        :player lemon:marker :by .
```

Note that we have specified the sense as being composed of several subsenses: the class Goal, the property leadsTo specifying that there is some action that led to the goal, and the property byPlayer specifying that the action was executed by the player that in the syntactic structure is expressed as a possessive adjunct. The complex sense in lines 7–15 thus relates the subject argument, the goal, to the possessive argument, the player that executed a soccer event which led to that goal. This is a good example of a mismatch between the domain modeling and natural language. (We will introduce a different solution, which accommodates the domain-independent flavor of the preposition by, in Chapter 7.)

The grammar entry for goal by would then look as follows:

98.

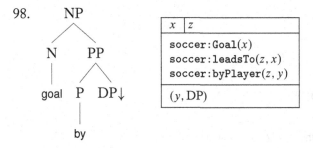

So far we can compose a goal by Drogba. Let us look at the expression in the third minute, which we already discussed in Chapter 3 on page 41. There we argued that in the n minute should correspond to one grammar entry that semantically refers to the datatype property `atMinute` with object n. A lexical entry for this verbalization apparently is not one single word but a phrase composed of a preposition, a determiner and a noun, as shown in 99, which assumes additional entries for the elements of the decomposition list, i.e., for in, the and minute.

```
99. :inTheMinute a lemon:Phrase ;
       lemon:decomposition ( :in :the :num_arg :minute ) ;
       lemon:sense [ lemon:reference soccer:atMinute ;
                     lemon:objOfProp :num_arg ] .
```

Note that this structure only captures the prepositional phrase and does not determine whether it serves as an NP or VP adjunct. Usually both are possible, so the grammar generation process should construct both an NP and a VP adjunction tree. Also note that from the decomposition list, the grammar generation process will only be able to construct a flat tree structure instead of the tree on page 41.

For the numeral third, we assume the following simple, domain-independent grammar entry:

100. NUM

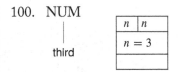

Now composing the whole DP a goal by Drogba in the third minute, and collapsing predicates $P(x, y)$ with equalities $y = a$ into $P(x, a)$, yields the following syntactic and semantic representations:

101.

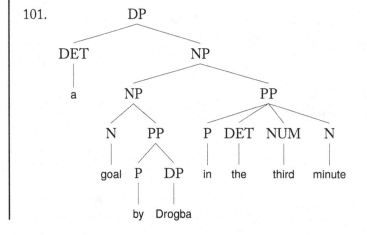

x	$x\,z$
soccer:Goal(x)	
soccer:leadsTo(z,x)	
soccer:byPlayer(z, soccer:DidierDrogba)	
soccer:atMinute($z,3$)	

So we have now composed Chelsea won as well as a goal by Drogba in the third minute. The only expression still missing is the connecting because of. This is obviously an expression that is independent of the domain. Syntactically it requires a noun phrase and then adjoins as an adverbial modifier to a verb phrase, as specified in the LTAG tree in 102. Semantically we could argue that it simply expresses a causal relation between a cause x and a consequence y, as in the DUDES in 102.

102.

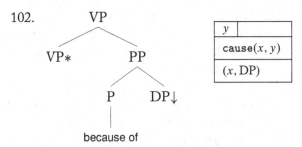

y	
cause(x,y)	
(x, DP)	

If we assume these representations for because of, composing it with Chelsea won and a goal by Drogba in the third minute yields the following final sentence meaning:

103.

	$y\,x\,z$
soccer:winner(y, soccer:ChelseaFC)	
cause(x,e)	
soccer:Goal(x)	
soccer:leadsTo(z,x)	
soccer:byPlayer(z, soccer:DidierDrogba)	
soccer:atMinute($z,3$)	

This captures quite well what the sentence 90 expresses. But there are parts of the meaning still left implicit, both by the sentence and its meaning representation, especially with respect to the state of affairs we depicted in 91 above. For example, we would understand that y is most probably a match and that the goal x happened in that very match. We as humans infer this from our knowledge about soccer, such as that you can win a game only by scoring goals in that game, not by means of goals in other games.

Exercise 6.2 Reproduce the steps from conceptualization to the composition of the sentence meaning with the following example. Enrich your ontology if necessary.

104. In a sold-out stadium the visiting team won a scoreless match.

Which meaning postulates would you need in order to capture the inconsistency of a team winning a match without goals?

6.2 CHALLENGES

When aligning syntactic and semantic representations to the underlying ontology, the most important question is what the units of composition are. Which complex expressions are regular and thus can be compositionally built from their parts? An example is early goal, where the noun goal refers to the ontology class of goals and is modified by the adjective early that expresses that some event or action happened, say, in the first 15 minutes of the game. And which complex expressions are irregular, i.e., have to be part of the lexicon because they cannot be built compositionally? An example is the prepositional phrase in the *n* minute, as we have seen before.

We have argued that the ontology should serve as a major guide in deciding which expressions are to be decomposed and which ones are not. If a concept is atomic in the ontology, the corresponding expression should be atomic in the grammar. Likewise, if an expression refers to a complex concept composed of several parts, then it should be composed from these parts. But this is not always possible. As an example, consider victory and defeat in combination with whether a team played in its home stadium or at another team's location:

104. (a) home victory

(b) away victory

(c) home defeat

(d) away defeat

The expressions in 104 are made up of two parts: victory or defeat, and home or away. Do these parts have a meaning with respect to the ontology?

Both home victory and away defeat means that there is a match that took place in the home stadium of the winner, while both home defeat and away victory means that there is a match that took place in the home stadium of the loser, where in one case the perspective is on the winner and in one case it is on the loser. We can thus specify the following meanings for home victory and home defeat in 105, where stadium relates a game to the stadium in which it took place, and homeArena relates a team to its home stadium.

105. home victory   home defeat

m	$w\ s$
soccer:Match(m)	
soccer:winner(m, w)	
soccer:stadium(m, s)	
soccer:homeArena(w, s)	

m	$l\ s$
soccer:Match(m)	
soccer:loser(m, l)	
soccer:stadium(m, s)	
soccer:homeArena(l, s)	

The meaning representations for away victory and away defeat could be the same, although we lose the expressions' perspective on the winner or loser.

So it seems that we can indeed compose the meaning of the whole from the meanings of its parts: The match with the winner or loser comes from victory and defeat, while the modifiers home and away contribute the home arena in relation to the stadium where the game took place. Let us try. As grammar entries for victory and defeat we can straightforwardly assume the following:

106. (a) NP

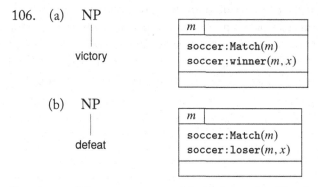

            victory

m	
soccer:Match(m)	
soccer:winner(m, x)	

(b) NP

            defeat

m	
soccer:Match(m)	
soccer:loser(m, x)	

For the modifier home, we would need an entry like the following:

107. NP

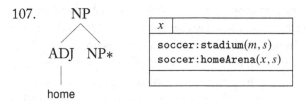

ADJ   NP*

    home

x	
soccer:stadium(m, s)	
soccer:homeArena(x, s)	

Here we assume that the predicate `stadium` is part of the meaning of home, although this excludes combinations like home team. Leaving out this predicate would require us to infer that missing part of the meaning representation. But in either case, there is a much more immediate problem with 107. We assumed that the main referent of the meaning representations of victory and defeat in 106 is m, as these nouns denote a match. This way the main variable of the meaning representation of home, x, would be unified with m, although x is actually needed to be unified with the winning or losing team. There are only two options to fix this. Either we assume that victory and defeat select the modifier as an argument. But this we do not want for syntactic reasons, as it contradicts our understanding of a modifier and forces us to specify different trees for all usages of these nouns: without modifiers, with a modifier, maybe also with two or more modifiers. Or we assume that the main referent of the meaning representations of victory and defeat is x. This we do not want for semantic reasons, because then unification with the meaning representations of other modifiers, such as in 3-0 victory, would yield wrong results.

Things get even worse with away. The grammar entry would look very much like 107, but the main referent x would need to unify with the loser in case of 106a and with the winner in case of 106b. Although it would not be a problem to specify also the other team as y in the meaning representations in 106, we would also need to determine that in the case of home, unification with x is carried out, while in the case of away unification with y is carried out.

So there is no feasible way to compositionally connect the meanings of home and away with the meanings of victory and defeat. We therefore have to assume grammar entries for the compounds, fixing their meaning as in 105. This is mainly due to the particular way we decided to model stadiums, matches and their winners and losers. Of course we could now decide to adapt the ontology, so it is closer to the conceptualization underlying natural language. But often ontology engineering and lexicon creation are separate processes, carried out by different persons.

A slightly different challenge that also arises from our specific domain conceptualization is the following. In 95 above, we captured the transitive and intransitive usage of the verb to win by specifying a lexical entry with two syntactic behaviors. The following case of to score looks very similar but turns out to be quite challenging:

108.   (a) Cantona scored.

    (b) Cantona scored a goal.

    (c) Cantona scored a penalty kick.

Syntactically the situation is exactly as with win, as the verb can be used both in intransitive and transitive contexts. Semantically the situation is more complex. Let us start by looking at the sentence meanings. All three sentences mean that Cantona is the agent of a soccer action that led to a goal. That goal is explicitly mentioned in the second sentence and remains implicit in the first and third one. The soccer action, on the other hand, is mentioned explicitly in the third sentence, while it remains implicit in the first two. Focusing on the transitive usage only, the representations in 109a and 109b are the ones needed for interpreting the transitive sentences in 108b and 108c, respectively.

109. (a)

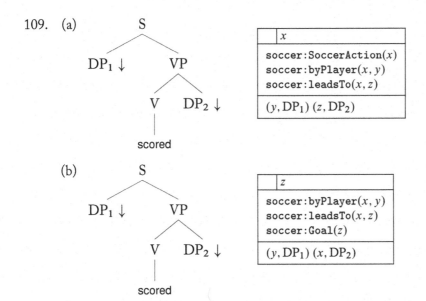

The above representations pose a problem: In 109a the object DP contributes the goal, while in 109b the object DP contributes the soccer action. Syntactically, there is no way to distinguish between the two entries, so when composing the meaning of scored with the meaning of the object argument, how does the interpretation process know which of the two DUDES to pick?

Given the machinery introduced so far, there is no answer yet. However, when developing tools for dealing with ambiguities and vague expressions in the next chapter, we will come across a solution.

CHAPTER 7

Ontological Reasoning for Ambiguity Resolution

There is a range of different kinds of inferences that play a role in the interpretation of natural language. However, most of them are too big a subject to satisfactorily treat them in one chapter. Therefore we will focus on one particular phenomenon where ontological reasoning can help us: the resolution of ambiguities. This chapter explores different ways of representing ambiguities and in particular how reasoning can be used to resolve them. This provides a first step toward exploiting meaning representations for automatically drawing inferences. While a deeper look into a wider range of inferences is beyond the scope of the book, this chapter aims at demonstrating that the way toward such investigations is paved.

7.1 AMBIGUITIES IN THE CONTEXT OF ONTOLOGY-BASED INTERPRETATION

Ambiguities comprise all cases in which natural language expressions have more than one meaning. This can be due to alternative lexical meanings, structural properties, or a combination of both.

The classic example of a lexical ambiguity is the noun bank, denoting either a financial institution or a bank of a river. In 110 the linguistic context together with world knowledge allows us to conclude that in the following sentence the meaning as a financial institution is meant:

110. The star player deposited his money at the bank.

Ambiguities arising from structural properties are often due to various potential attachment sites for modifiers. For example, wooden ball container can either be a wooden container for balls or a container for wooden balls, depending on which noun phrase the adjective wooden adjoins to. Analogously, peaceful supporters and ultras either includes only peaceful ultras or all ultras independent of their disposition. The same kind of ambiguities arise from different attachment sites for prepositional phrases, as in 111.

111. (a) James Bond shot the man with the golden gun.

    (b) Put the ball on the table by the window in the kitchen.

Another case of structural ambiguities is scope ambiguities, as discussed in Section 3.7.

In the context of ontology-based interpretation, we understand the term *ambiguity* as comprising all cases in which a natural language expression does not correspond uniquely to one ontology concept but rather can correspond to several—disjoint or overlapping—ontology concepts. The proclamation in 112a, for example, can talk about either Gerd Müller or Thomas Müller. And the noun capacity in the context of an extensive soccer ontology can, in a question like 112b, refer to either total capacity or seated capacity. In this case the ontology modeling is simply more fine-grained than the natural language expression.

112.   (a) What a marvelous pass by Müller!

(b) Which stadiums have a capacity greater than 60,000?

Another case of expressions that can correspond to several ontology concepts are vague and semantically light expressions, and we will here extend the term *ambiguity* to also cover those. An example for a vague expression is the adjective big, which usually refers to size. In 113a this means body height, while in 113b this can be size with respect to either capacity or dimension.

113.   (a) Who is the biggest goal keeper?

(b) What is the biggest stadium?

Examples of semantically light expressions are verbs such as to be and to have, and prepositions such as with, of, and in. Consider with in the following examples:

114.   (a) the team with the best players

(b) the match with the most goals

In order to construct appropriate meaning representations for these noun phrases, with in 114a has to correspond to the ontology property playsFor, relating players with teams, while in 114b it has to correspond to the property inMatch, relating goals with the match they occur in. Analogous expressions involving the verb to have can be found in an expression such as Brazil has the best players. Note that in these examples the linguistic context together with the domain and range restrictions of the ontology properties admit only one of the alternative interpretations. This, however, is not always the case. Possessives are a good example:

115. Berti's team always loses.

The possessive here indicates that there is some relationship between Berti and the team, but which one is not specified. It could be the team that Berti plays for, the one that he is coach of, or maybe even the one he is supporting, to name just a few possibilities.

Ambiguous expressions are pervasive. Selecting BBC articles about matches of the European championship 2012, we found that almost 10% of the words are vague expressions (prepositions like with, of, for, possessives, etc.), occurring in roughly 60–80% of all sentences. So if we do not have a way to deal with them in the automatic interpretation process, we would fail to construct meaning representations in a significant amount of cases.

In order to deal with ambiguous expressions, we first need a way to represent ambiguities. Until now our meaning representations contain individuals and predicates corresponding to specific ontology concepts, but what should we specify as semantic representations of ambiguous expression such as big and with? Further, we need a way to resolve ambiguities. In fact, although ambiguous expressions are pervasive, sentences usually have one intended meaning in a given context, and we as humans are quite good at grasping that meaning to an extent that sometimes we even fail to even notice ambiguities [Poesio and Reyle, 2001].

7.2 REPRESENTING AND RESOLVING AMBIGUITIES

When constructing a semantic representation, we want to capture all possible meaning alternatives. There are roughly two strategies to achieve this. On the one hand, we could construct a representation for every meaning alternative, thus enumerating all those alternatives. On the other hand, we could construct an underspecified representation that subsumes all meaning alternatives in one single representation. We will consider and contrast both strategies in the following.

7.2.1 ENUMERATION

Consider the following examples with the adjective big:

116.   (a) a big goal keeper

       (b) a big stadium

We mentioned that generally big refers to size: in the first example this means size with respect to body height, while in the second example it means size with respect to capacity or dimension. There are even more meaning alternatives, of course, but let us consider only height and capacity for the moment. In order to enumerate both, we would need the following two grammar entries.

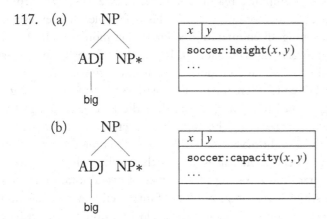

The syntactic representation is the same in both cases and only the semantic representation differs. It refers to the relation height in the first case and to capacity in the second case. Additionally, the value y has to lie above some threshold which depends on both the relation and its domain (recall the discussion of scalar adjectives in Chapter 4). We gloss over this part of the modeling here as it does not play a role for ambiguities.

When composing noun phrases as in 116, the interpretation process has two entries for big at its disposal and no way to favor one over the other a priori. Enumerating all possibilities means that both entries will be used, leading to two different interpretations. For a big goalkeeper this yields the two interpretations in 118a (displaying only the relevant part and glossing over the threshold), and for a big stadium this yields the two interpretations in 118b (again only displaying the relevant part and glossing over the threshold).

118.   (a)

x	$x\ y$
soccer:height(x, y)	
soccer:Goalkeeper(x)	
...	

x	$x\ y$
soccer:capacity(x, y)	
soccer:Goalkeeper(x)	
...	

(b)

x	$x\ y$
soccer:height(x, y)	
soccer:Stadium(x)	
...	

x	$x\ y$
soccer:capacity(x, y)	
soccer:Stadium(x)	
...	

Having a closer look at the interpretation alternatives we see that both in 118a and 118b only one of them makes sense with respect to the ontology. The other one violates domain restrictions by attributing a capacity, a property of stadiums, to a person and by attributing a height, a property of persons, to stadiums. So although we capture two possible meaning alternatives, we also capture two impossible ones.

Therefore, a necessary next step is to employ a reasoner in order to filter out all interpretations that are inconsistent with respect to the ontology. While this is feasible, this represents a quite brute-forth approach. When running an enumeration approach on more than 600 user questions over a geographical domain [Unger and Cimiano, 2011a], we found that on average a question had five meaning representations, with an enormous standard deviation: some queries had up to 96 representations, almost all of which were inconsistent with respect to the ontology.

So how about not constructing inconsistent interpretations in the first place but rather filtering them out as early as possible, thereby reducing the number of interpretations during the course of meaning composition? A quite straightforward way to do so is to employ the reasoner at each step of the interpretation process to check the consistency of the result, such that at every step inconsistent combinations are filtered out, reducing the number of overall interpretations early on. For the geographical user questions, the average number of interpretations per question would drop to three and a half, and even more significantly the majority of questions actually ends up with only one interpretation, some with two, three, or four, but hardly any with more, the maximum number of interpretations being ten.

7.2.2 UNDERSPECIFICATION

One problem, however, remains. Take the preposition with, as in the example 114 above, repeated here:

119. (a) the team with the best players

(b) the match with the most goals

In Chapter 4 we mentioned that closed-class expressions like prepositions should not be part of a domain lexicon, as they are used across all domains. However, in a particular sentence they do acquire a domain-specific meaning. In the first example in 119, for instance, with expresses the relation playsFor, while in the second example it expresses the relation inMatch. If we do not want to encode these meanings in the domain lexicon, and consequently in the domain grammar, how do we capture them?

Even if we decided to capture the above meaning alternatives in some lexicon or grammar part, this would raise a new problem. The above are only two of many meaning alternatives; here are a few more possible contexts of use in which the preposition with can occur in the soccer domain:

120. (a) the stadium with the most seats

(b) the player with the most red cards

(c) the team with the most titles

(d) the team with the oldest stadium

Each of them would require with to refer to a different ontological relation. We bet you we could even construct sentences for all relations in our ontology such that with expresses the relation in question. The same holds for the semantically light verb to have and some other expressions. Consequently, if we have, for example, twenty properties in our ontology, we would need to specify twenty different meaning alternatives for those expressions. And as soon as we remove or add a property, we need to change this set of meanings accordingly.

This leads us to the second strategy we had mentioned in the beginning of the section: underspecification. Instead of having to specify two, five, ten or twenty meaning alternatives, we will specify one meaning that subsumes all, in the case of closed-class expressions even one that is domain-independent.

In order to subsume several meaning alternatives in one semantic representation, we introduce metavariables $\mathcal{P}, \mathcal{R}, \ldots$ over predicates. Further, we enrich semantic representations with restrictions on the instantiation of those metavariables with actual ontology predicates. They take the following general form, expressing that $\mathcal{P}$ can be instantiated by property p_1 if x belongs to class c_i and y belongs to class c_j (and possibly additional class restrictions on other variables), and it can be instantiated by property p_n if x belongs to class c_k, y belongs to class c_l, and so on:

$$\mathcal{P} \mapsto p_1(x = c_i, y = c_j, \ldots)$$
$$| \ldots$$
$$| p_n(x = c_k, y = c_l \ldots)$$

The two meaning representations for the adjective big, for example, as given in 121a, can be combined into the single meaning representation given in 121b, expressing that big denotes some property that is either `height`, if its first argument belongs to the class `Person`, or `capacity`, if its first argument belongs to the class `Stadium`.

121.   (a)

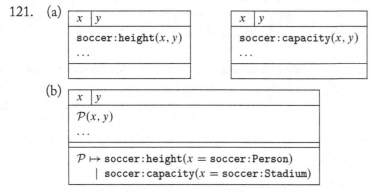

(b)

When constructing a meaning representation for the noun phrases a big goalkeeper and a big stadium, the interpretation process does not specify four alternatives, as before, but only one, 122a for the former and 122b for the latter:

122.   (a)

(b)

As soon as the argument x is provided, the metavariable can be resolved to exactly those instantiations that are consistent with the ontology. To this end, we invoke a reasoner that checks the satisfiability of the intersection of x's type information with the instantiation restrictions. The type of x is extracted from the conditions `soccer:Goalkeeper(x)` and `soccer:Stadium(x)`. If the meaning representation does not contain such predicates, the type can often be inferred from domain and range restrictions of properties. For example, if x would occur in a condition `soccer:byPlayer(z, x)`, from the range restriction of the property `byPlayer` it would follow that x is a player.

In the case of 122a this leads to the following satisfiability checks:

- `Person ⊓ Goalkeeper` is satisfiable, as the latter is a subclass of the former; thus `height` is a consistent instantiation of $\mathcal{P}$

- `Person ⊓ Stadium` is not satisfiable, as these classes are defined to be disjoint; thus `capacity` is not a consistent instantiation of $\mathcal{P}$

So there is exactly one consistent interpretation and we can resolve the metavariable, yielding the following specified representation:

123.

x	$x\ y\ z$
`soccer:height(`x, y`)`	
...	
`soccer:Goalkeeper(`x`)`	

Analogously, in 122b the metavariable $\mathcal{P}$ can be resolved to `capacity`.

Of course, it could also be that more than one interpretation is consistent with the ontology. In that case the semantic representation remains underspecified unless it can finally be resolved, possibly to more than one admissible meaning alternatives at the end of the derivation. In case none of the instantiations of a metavariable is consistent with the ontology, the interpretation aborts without a meaning representation. We invite you to reconstruct these cases in detail with the following exercise.

Exercise 7.1   Given three meaning alternatives for big denoting size with respect to height (of a person), capacity or dimension (of a stadium, such as Wembley and Camp Nou, two of the most iconic soccer stadiums), build all consistent meaning representations for the following examples, if any:

124.   (a) Wembley is bigger than Camp Nou.

(b) Wembley is bigger than Arminia Bielefeld.

Let us turn to closed-class expressions, especially prepositions like with and the semantically light auxiliary verb to have. We have argued that these expressions are used across all domains and therefore should not be part of a domain lexicon and grammar. Can we assign them a domain-independent meaning representation then? Recall the discussion about with above. We have seen that with can refer to pretty much any ontological relation, very much like to have. Since they are underspecified with respect to the relation they refer to in a specific context, we represent their semantic content by means of a metavariable. But instead of listing all relations as possible instantiations, we simply do not give any instantiation restriction at all and leave it to the reasoner to find all consistent instantiations. A grammar entry for the preposition with, for example, can be specified as follows:

124.

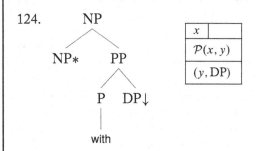

The task of the reasoner is to find all those ontological relations that admit the type of x or a superclass thereof as domain of the relation and the type of y or a superclass thereof as range of the relation.

Exercise 7.2   Specify a domain-independent grammar entry for the verb to have and construct all possible meaning representations for the following sentence.

125.   (a) The team with the big goalkeeper won.

(b) The defender already has a yellow card.

Hint: If you cannot figure out a semantic contribution of already, simply represent it as a grammar entry with an empty DUDES.

One thing still remains to be done. At the end of the previous chapter we promised to find a solution for the to score problem. Recall that to score could be used transitively in two different contexts: to score a goal and to score a penalty kick. We found that we need two slightly different meaning representations, given in 109 on page 105 and repeated here:

125.

x	
$\texttt{soccer:SoccerAction}(x)$	
$\texttt{soccer:byPlayer}(x, y)$	
$\texttt{soccer:leadsTo}(x, z)$	
$(y, \mathrm{DP}_1)\,(z, \mathrm{DP}_2)$	

z	
$\texttt{soccer:byPlayer}(x, y)$	
$\texttt{soccer:leadsTo}(x, z)$	
$\texttt{soccer:Goal}(z)$	
$(y, \mathrm{DP}_1)\,(x, \mathrm{DP}_2)$	

Can we find one underspecified meaning representation that subsumes both? It is a challenge, but we strongly encourage you to try before you read on.

Here is one possible solution, which works if we assume that the relation byPlayer relates both soccer actions and goals to a player:

126.

z
soccer:byPlayer(x, y) soccer:Goal(z) $\mathcal{P}(x, z)$
$(y, \mathrm{DP}_1)\ (x, \mathrm{DP}_2)$
$\mathcal{P} \mapsto$ soccer:leadsTo$(x =$ soccer:SoccerAction$)$ $\mid$ equals$(x =$ soccer:Goal$)$

Note that these instantiation restrictions distinguish both interpretations because the classes Goal and SoccerAction are disjoint in our ontology. If this were not the case, we would need to be more specific and restrict x to the class PenaltyKick—or, a bit more general, to the union of PenaltyKick, FreeKick and all other actions that you can score from.

Exercise 7.3   Check your and/or our underspecified representation by constructing interpretations for the example sentences from the previous chapter:

127.　(a) Cantona scored a goal.

　　　(b) Cantona scored a penalty kick.

This concludes our treatment of ambiguities. Their resolution with the help of ontological reasoning of course constitutes only a first step for exploiting a reasoner in the interpretation process, but, as is commonly known, every journey starts with a first step.

7.3   FURTHER READING

An overview of types of ambiguities and how they can be represented is given by Bunt [1995]. There has been a lot of research on the underspecification of scope ambiguities, introducing various formalisms such as Underspecified Discourse Representation Theory [Reyle, 1993, 1995], Hole Semantics [Bos, 1995], Minimal Recursion Semantics [Copestake et al., 2005] and Dominance Constraints [Koller et al., 2003]. A standard approach for representing lexical ambiguities is to introduce a *metaconstant* that can be bound to the appropriate meaning of a lexical element in context (see Bunt [1995]). This is essentially what we do in our approach. Hobbs et al. have also proposed metaconstants to underspecify the relation between nouns in a nominal compound [Hobbs et al., 1993]. Cimiano and Reyle [2003] have proposed a formalism that allows exploiting ontological knowledge to resolve ambiguities in context. Concerning the resolution of ambiguities, there has been a lot of research on the task of *word sense disambiguation* [Ide and Véronis,

1998], i.e., the task of determining the appropriate meaning of a word in context. The semantics of lexical underspecification is analyzed in more depth by Pustejovsky [2009] and the relation between vagueness, ambiguity and underspecification is discussed by Pinkal [1996]. An approach to the resolution of lexical ambiguities based on *polaroid words* was presented by Hirst [1987]. Statistical approaches to solving syntactic ambiguities (e.g., prepositional attachment) have also been proposed early on (see e.g., Hindle and Rooth [1993]).

CHAPTER 8

Temporal Interpretation

Temporal aspects are fundamental to natural language interpretation. In fact, one could even go as far as stating that there is no sentence or utterance the interpretation of which does not involve temporal aspects. Thus, our approach to ontology-based interpretation of natural language has to account for these temporal aspects. For this purpose, we need an ontology or logical vocabulary that allows us to represent the temporal aspects of the meaning of a sentence, utterance or discourse. Instead of developing our own ontology, we will build on the *time ontology* [Hobbs and Pan, 2004]. While this ontology is available in OWL, it is not deeply axiomatized. In fact, many axioms in the time ontology cannot be represented in OWL 2 DL and would require full first-order logic if not higher-order logics. In this chapter, we thus focus on a first-order axiomatization of the concepts and properties in the OWL version of the time ontology.[1] We introduce the essential ontological predicates defined in the time ontology first and then show how a large variety of temporal expressions can be interpreted with respect to the vocabulary provided by the time ontology.

8.1 THE TIME ONTOLOGY

As a starter, consider the following three utterances:

127. (a) The deciding goal was scored in the 90th minute.

    (b) Vogts took over as coach of the German team after Beckenbauer.

    (c) How often did Bhutan win during the 1990s?

We can already capture the meaning of the first sentence, as our soccer ontology contains a relation atMinute, specifying the minute of the game at which a soccer event happens. However, this only works as long as we are talking about game minutes and not in absolute terms, like in The deciding goal was scored at 21:05. Especially the other two examples show that we need a means to talk about time beyond game minutes.

Following our ontology-based approach to the interpretation of natural language, we want to capture temporal aspects in an ontology. So what do we need such a time ontology to cover? It should define time points, so we can refer to the time point when a goal or some other event happens, and it should define time intervals, so we can refer to a decade like the 1990s or the time span of someone being coach. And in addition, it should define relations between time points and

---

[1]A partial OWL axiomatization of the time ontology can be found on the book website.

intervals. The *time ontology* [Hobbs and Pan, 2004] does exactly that: it introduces both temporal entities and relations between them. In the following, we will take a detailed look at those entities and relations.

8.1.1 TEMPORAL ENTITIES AND THEIR ORDERING

First of all, the time ontology distinguishes Instants and Intervals as the two kinds of temporal entities, and defines them to be disjoint:

$$\forall x \, (\text{Instant}(x) \rightarrow \text{TemporalEntity}(x))$$

$$\forall x \, (\text{Interval}(x) \rightarrow \text{TemporalEntity}(x))$$

$$\forall x \, (\text{TemporalEntity}(x) \rightarrow \text{Instant}(x) \vee \text{Interval}(x))$$

$$\forall x \, (\text{Instant}(x) \rightarrow \neg\text{Interval}(x))$$

Intuitively, intervals are temporal entities that have a temporal extension, while instants are point-like and have no extension.

Temporal intervals can have a beginning and an end, but they do not have to, i.e., they can have an infinite duration. The time ontology distinguishes between *positively infinite* intervals, which have no end, and *negatively infinite* intervals, which have no starting point. The begins and ends predicates relate time instants to the time intervals they begin or end:

$$\forall t, T \, (\text{begins}(t, T) \rightarrow \text{Instant}(t) \wedge \text{TemporalEntity}(T))$$

$$\forall t, T \, (\text{ends}(t, T) \rightarrow \text{Instant}(t) \wedge \text{TemporalEntity}(T))$$

Here and in the following we use the lower-case letter t to represent an instant, and the upper-case letter T to represent an interval. In particular, an instant is the beginning and end of itself:

$$\forall t (\text{Instant}(t) \rightarrow \text{begins}(t, t))$$

$$\forall t (\text{Instant}(t) \rightarrow \text{ends}(t, t))$$

If they exist, beginnings and ends are unique, i.e., begins and ends are functional:

$$\forall t_1, t_2, T \, (\text{begins}(t_1, T) \wedge \text{begins}(t_2, T) \rightarrow t_1 = t_2)$$

$$\forall t_1, t_2, T \, (\text{ends}(t_1, T) \wedge \text{ends}(t_2, T) \rightarrow t_1 = t_2)$$

So far we can talk about time points and time intervals, but something crucial is still missing: a means to express that some time point or interval is before or after another. To this end, we assume the availability of a total order before between instants. On the basis of this total order, we can define a relation before between temporal intervals as follows:

$$\forall T_1, T_2 \, (\text{before}(T_1, T_2) \leftrightarrow \exists t_1, t_2 \, (\text{ends}(t_1, T_1) \wedge \text{begins}(t_2, T_2) \wedge \text{before}(t_1, t_2)))$$

The relation before between intervals is anti-reflexive, anti-symmetric and transitive:

$$\forall T_1, T_2 \, (\texttt{before}(T_1, T_2) \rightarrow T_1 \neq T_2)$$

$$\forall T_1, T_2 \, (\texttt{before}(T_1, T_2) \rightarrow \neg \texttt{before}(T_2, T_1))$$

$$\forall T_1, T_2, T_3 \, (\texttt{before}(T_1, T_2) \wedge \texttt{before}(T_2, T_3) \rightarrow \texttt{before}(T_1, T_3))$$

Finally, we can define after as the inverse relation of before:

$$\forall t_1, t_2 \, (\texttt{before}(t_1, t_2) \leftrightarrow \texttt{after}(t_2, t_1))$$

When considering the axioms for intervals that we have introduced above, we see that it is still possible that the beginning and end of an interval is the same time point. In such a case, an interval has no extension. In order to talk about intervals that do have an extension, we define *proper intervals* to be intervals whose beginning and end point is not the same:

$$\forall T \, (\texttt{ProperInterval}(T) \leftrightarrow \texttt{Interval}(T) \wedge$$
$$\forall t_1, t_2 \, (\texttt{begins}(t_1, T) \wedge \texttt{ends}(t_2, T) \rightarrow t_1 \neq t_2))$$

Further, the following two statements about intervals hold. First, the end of an interval is not before the beginning of the interval (but could be the same):

$$\forall T, t_1, t_2 \, (\texttt{Interval}(T) \wedge \texttt{begins}(t_1, T) \wedge \texttt{ends}(t_2, T) \rightarrow \neg \texttt{before}(t_2, t_1))$$

And second, more specifically, the beginning of a proper interval is before the end of the interval (i.e., could not be the same):

$$\forall T, t_1, t_2 \, (\texttt{ProperInterval}(T) \wedge \texttt{begins}(t_1, T) \wedge \texttt{ends}(t_2, T) \rightarrow \texttt{before}(t_1, t_2))$$

A special relation between time points and intervals is inside, expressing that some time point is in the extension of an interval, which is defined as follows:

$$\forall T, t, t_1, t_2 \, (\texttt{inside}(t, T) \wedge \texttt{begins}(t_1, T) \wedge \texttt{ends}(t_2, T) \wedge \texttt{ProperInterval}(T)$$
$$\rightarrow \texttt{before}(t_1, t) \wedge \texttt{before}(t, t_2))$$

This provides us with a basic vocabulary to talk about time points and intervals, the beginning and end of an interval, and the order between those temporal entities. However, we still cannot talk about specific relations between intervals, for example expressing that someone was coach of a team during the 1990s.

8.1.2 TEMPORAL RELATIONS

Following Allen and Ferguson's interval calculus [Allen, 1984; Allen and Ferguson, 1997], Hobbs and Pan define a number of temporal relations between proper intervals. We provide only an intuitive description of these temporal relations in what follows. For details and the appropriate axiomatization, the interested reader is referred to Hobbs and Pan [2004].

- `intEquals`: A proper interval T_1 equals another interval T_2 if they have the same start and end point.

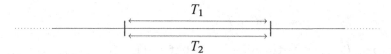

- `intBefore`: A proper interval T_1 is before a proper interval T_2 if the end of T_1 is before the start of T_2.

- `intMeets`: A proper interval T_1 meets a proper interval T_2 if the end of T_1 corresponds to the start of T_2.

- `intOverlaps`: A proper interval T_1 overlaps with a proper interval T_2 if T_2 begins before T_1 ends, T_1 starts before T_2 does, and T_2 ends after T_1 does.

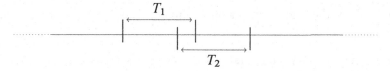

- `intStarts`: A proper interval T_1 starts a proper interval T_2 if they start at the same time, and the end of T_1 is before the end of T_2 (if it has one).

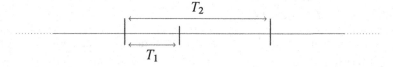

- `intDuring`: A proper interval T_1 is during (or is contained in) an interval T_2 if T_1 has a start and an end and the start of T_1 is after the start of T_2 (if it has one) and the end of T_1 is before the end of T_2 (if it has one).

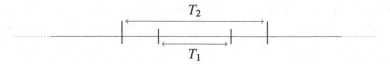

- `intFinishes`: A proper interval T_1 finishes another proper interval T_2 if both end at the same time, and the start of T_1 (if it has one) is after the start of T_2.

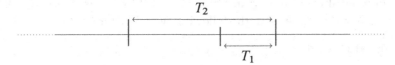

In terms of these relations, also the following inverse relations can be defined:

$$\forall T_1, T_2 \,(\texttt{intAfter}(T_1, T_2) \leftrightarrow \texttt{intBefore}(T_2, T_1))$$

$$\forall T_1, T_2 \,(\texttt{intMetBy}(T_1, T_2) \leftrightarrow \texttt{intMeets}(T_2, T_1))$$

$$\forall T_1, T_2 \,(\texttt{intOverlappedBy}(T_1, T_2) \leftrightarrow \texttt{intOverlaps}(T_2, T_1))$$

$$\forall T_1, T_2 \,(\texttt{intStartedBy}(T_1, T_2) \leftrightarrow \texttt{intStarts}(T_2, T_1))$$

$$\forall T_1, T_2 \,(\texttt{intContains}(T_1, T_2) \leftrightarrow \texttt{intDuring}(T_2, T_1))$$

$$\forall T_1, T_2 \,(\texttt{intFinishedBy}(T_1, T_2) \leftrightarrow \texttt{intFinishes}(T_2, T_1))$$

This gives us the means to express that the time span of someone being coach of a team was during a specific interval, that some coach was the successor of someone else, and the like. But when talking about time, we are usually also talking about events happening at a certain time, be it a goal, the FIFA's introduction of a new rule, or a team winning the world championship. So in addition to temporal entities, there are various relations between events and the intervals and time points at which they hold. Hobbs and Pan distinguish the following relations:

- `atTime`, relating some event e with an instant t, expressing that e takes place at t.

- `during`, expressing that a certain event e takes place during the time interval T. This implies that the event e takes place at every interval and instant inside of T:

$$\forall e, T \,(\texttt{during}(e, T) \wedge \texttt{inside}(t, T) \rightarrow \texttt{atTime}(e, t))$$

$$\forall e, T_1, T_2 \,(\texttt{during}(e, T_1) \wedge \texttt{intDuring}(T_2, T_1) \rightarrow \texttt{during}(e, T_2))$$

- `holds`, used to express that a certain event takes place during an interval or time point.

So we can express that an event happened during a particular interval, but how would we express that this interval corresponds to the the 1990s?

8.1.3 THE STRUCTURE OF TIME

Time intervals have a duration that can be measured with respect to some unit of measurement, e.g., the duration of an interval could be a year, two hours, or 47 seconds. For this, the time ontology introduces a relation duration with the following type signature:

$$\text{duration}: \text{Interval} \times \text{TemporalUnit} \rightarrow \mathbb{R} \cup \{\infty\}$$

TemporalUnit comprises the *clock intervals* *Second*, *Minute* and *Hour*, and the *calender intervals* *Day*, *Month* and *Year*, and ∞ is allowed in order to be able to express the duration of intervals without beginning or end.

For example, the duration of the interval [19:14, 19:17] in minutes would be 3, i.e., duration([19:14, 19:17], *Minute*) = 3, while in seconds it would be 180, i.e., duration([19:14, 19:17], *Second*) = 180. This allows for the introduction of special functions that return the duration of an interval in terms of some given unit, for instance seconds(T) = duration(T, *Second*), and for the definition of conversion rules between such predicates, such as seconds(T) = 60 * minutes(T).

An indication of the duration of an interval, however, does not say much about the internal structure of an interval. In the domain of time, an interval is typically constituted by a set of consequent intervals of the same length, i.e., a minute is constituted by 60 consequent intervals of the duration of a second, a week is constituted of seven consequent intervals of the duration of a day, and so on. The time ontology defines a relation Hath to express this. For example, given that T is an interval corresponding to the month September of some year, then Hath(30, *Day*, T) would be true.

In natural language, most of the time we refer to so-called calendar and clock intervals. The time ontology defines special relations to single out calendar and clock intervals from larger intervals. For example, a calendar day differs from other intervals of length *Day* in that it starts at minute 0:00 and ends at minute 23:59. To capture this, the special predicate calInt(y, n, u, x) states that the interval y is the n-th calendar interval of unit length u within interval x. For example, it holds that calInt(12-March-2002, 12, *Day*, March-2002). Analogously, the predicate clockInt(y, n, u, x) states that y is the n-th clock interval of unit length u within interval x. This allows for the definition of a range of predicates to single out the n-th second, minute and hour using clockInt, and the n-th day, month and year using calInt within a larger interval. We exemplify this for minutes, days and weeks, the rest is analogous:

$$\forall y, n, x \, (\text{min}(y, n, x) \leftrightarrow \text{clockInt}(y, n, *\text{Minute}*, x))$$
$$\forall y, n, x \, (\text{da}(y, n, x) \leftrightarrow \text{calInt}(y, n, *\text{Day}*, x))$$
$$\forall y, n, x \, (\text{wk}(y, n, x) \leftrightarrow \text{calInt}(y, n, *\text{Week}*, x))$$

Exercise 8.1 Define the interval that spans the 1990s.

8.2 TEMPORAL INTERPRETATION WITH RESPECT TO THE TIME ONTOLOGY

The temporal predicates we have at hand now allow us to build meaning representations that incorporate temporal aspects. So how can we specify the semantics of past, present and future tense? Assuming that tense is a verb modifier and giving only a very rough, insufficient account of the morphological operations involved, we can specify the following syntactic and semantic representations, where the latter specify that the event expressed by the verb holds at an interval T that is during, before or after another interval T_0 containing the specific time point now:[2]

128. (a) *Present tense:*

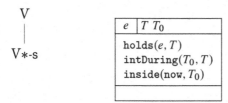

(b) *Past tense:*

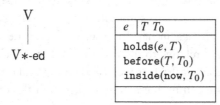

(c) *Future tense:*

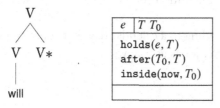

The sentence Arminia Bielefeld will win therefore has the interpretation given in 131, when combining the future tense meaning representation in 128c with the meaning representations of Arminia Bielefeld and win, given in 129 and 130, respectively.

129.

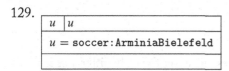

---

[2]We leave it open how this time point is determined. In a dialogue it could be the time of speaking, for a program interpreting written text it could be the system time, and so on.

130.

z	z
soccer:Match(z)	
soccer:winner(z, x)	
(DP, x)	

131.

	$z\ x\ T\ T_0$
soccer:Match(z)	
soccer:winner(z, x)	
x = soccer:ArminiaBielefeld	
holds(z, T)	
after(T_0, T)	
inside(now, T_0)	

Let us now turn to some of the most interesting (and also very commonly used) temporal expressions, namely those that express a time relative to some other time point. Examples are today, tomorrow, yesterday, this year, next week, and last month. In order to define the semantics of such expressions, we will fix their interpretation relative to the time point now, which is the time point at which the expression to be interpreted is uttered, as well as to an interval c that fixes the right unbounded interval corresponding to the common era relative to which the utterance was produced. This c represents the encompassing interval in predicates $\text{calInt}(y, n, u, c)$, expressing that y is the n-th interval of unit length u in the common era. We can then represent the semantics of yesterday, today and tomorrow as follows.

Today denotes that interval T_0 corresponding to a calendar day that contains the time point now. A grammar entry for today as VP modifier looks as follows:

132.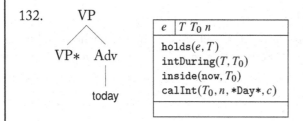

Note that part of the meaning is the same as for the present tense; the only difference is that the meaning of today is more specific by requiring T_0 to be of unit length *Day*. The interpretation of a sentence like Arminia Bielefeld wins today would thus be the following:

133.

z x T' T_0' T T_0 n
soccer:Match(z)
soccer:winner(z, x)
x = soccer:ArminiaBielefeld
holds(z, T)
intDuring(T, T_0)
inside(now, T_0)
holds(z, T')
intDuring(T', T_0')
inside(now, T_0')
calInt($T_0', n,$ *Day*, c)

We hope it is clear that the duplicate predicates could be left out without significantly changing the truth conditions of the semantic representation.

Yesterday denotes that interval T_{-1} corresponding to a calendar day that precedes the calendar day that contains now:

134.

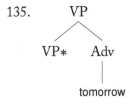

e	T T_0 T_{-1} n
holds(e, T)	
intDuring(T, T_{-1})	
calInt($T_0, n,$ *Day*, c)	
calInt($T_{-1}, n-1,$ *Day*, c)	
inside(now, T_0)	

Analogously, tomorrow denotes that interval T_{+1} corresponding to a calendar day that follows the calendar day that contains now:

135.

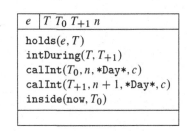

e	T T_0 T_{+1} n
holds(e, T)	
intDuring(T, T_{+1})	
calInt($T_0, n,$ *Day*, c)	
calInt($T_{+1}, n+1,$ *Day*, c)	
inside(now, T_0)	

Exercise 8.2 Construct interpretations for the following sentences and show why the last one is inconsistent:

136. (a) Arminia Bielefeld won yesterday.

  (b) Arminia Bielefeld will win tomorrow.

(c) Arminia Bielefeld won tomorrow.

Next, let us look at the meaning of the temporal operators next, last and this, in order to be able to compositionally build interpretations of expressions like last year, next Sunday, and so on. To this end, we assume the existence of a partial order between units as follows:

$$\text{*Second*} < \text{*Minute*} < \text{*Hour*} < \text{*Day*} < \text{*Week*} < \text{*Month*} < \text{*Year*}$$

Intuitively, next X refers to an interval T' of duration X that is contained in some (minimal) interval T_{+1} of unit length u such that the preceding interval T of unit length u contains now. For instance, next week refers to that interval T' of type *Week* that is contained in an interval T_{+1} of type *Week* such that the previous interval T of type *Week* contains now. Further, next thursday refers to that interval T' of type *Thursday* such that T' is contained in some (minimal) interval T_{+1} of type *Week* that does not contain now so that the preceding interval T of type *Week* contains now.

Syntactically, an expression like next behaves like a determiner, hence requires an NP argument. The syntactic and semantic representations of next can thus be formalized as follows. (We specify the representation for calInt, but it would look the same for clockInt).

136.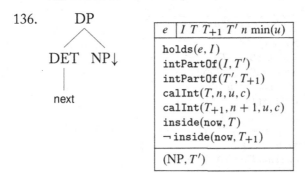

Here, $\texttt{intPartOf}(I, T')$ is a predicate that is true if $\texttt{intDuring}(I, T')$ or $\texttt{intEquals}(I, T')$ or $\texttt{intStarts}(I, T')$ or $\texttt{intFinishes}(I, T')$ is true. Further, $\min(u)$ binds the smallest u that satisfies all DRS conditions. In pure DRT terms, we would treat $\min(\cdot)$ by means of a quantifier; the DUDES would then contain a duplex condition (again see Section 3.7 in Chapter 3) in addition to the conditions of the above representation (now only indicated as ...), i.e., look like the following:

137.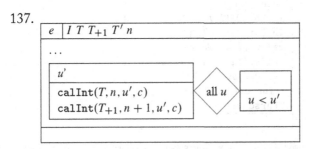

Nouns like day and Thursday constitute NPs with the meanings specified in the following, expressing that T' is a calender day (for day) and expressing that T' is the 5th interval of length day in some week (for Thursday).

138.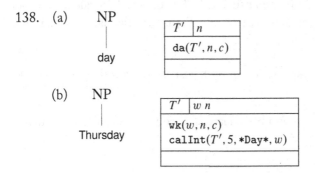

Combining next with those NPs would thus yield the following interpretations for next day (left) and next Thursday (right):

139.

e	$I\ T\ T_{+1}\ T'\ n\ \min(u)\ n'$
	$\mathrm{holds}(e, I)$
	$\mathrm{intPartOf}(I, T')$
	$\mathrm{intPartOf}(T', T_{+1})$
	$\mathrm{calInt}(T, n, u, c)$
	$\mathrm{calInt}(T_{+1}, n+1, u, c)$
	$\mathrm{inside}(\mathrm{now}, T)$
	$\neg\,\mathrm{inside}(\mathrm{now}, T_{+1})$
	$\mathrm{da}(T', n', c)$

e	$I\ T\ T_{+1}\ T'\ n\ \min(u)\ n'\ w$
	$\mathrm{holds}(e, I)$
	$\mathrm{intPartOf}(I, T')$
	$\mathrm{intPartOf}(T', T_{+1})$
	$\mathrm{calInt}(T, n, u, c)$
	$\mathrm{calInt}(T_{+1}, n+1, u, c)$
	$\mathrm{inside}(\mathrm{now}, T)$
	$\neg\,\mathrm{inside}(\mathrm{now}, T_{+1})$
	$\mathrm{wk}(w, n', c)$
	$\mathrm{calInt}(T', 5, \text{*Day*}, w)$

Since the minimal unit u that satisfies the conditions in the case of next day is *Day*, and in the case of next Thursday is *Week*, the above are equivalent to the following (abbreviating $\mathrm{wk}(w, n', c) \wedge \mathrm{calInt}(T', 5, \text{*Day*}, w)$ as $\mathrm{Thursday}(T')$):

140.

e	$I\ T\ T_{+1}\ T'\ n\ n'$
	$\mathrm{holds}(e, I)$
	$\mathrm{intPartOf}(I, T')$
	$\mathrm{calInt}(T, n, \text{*Day*}, c)$
	$\mathrm{calInt}(T_{+1}, n+1, \text{*Day*}, c)$
	$\mathrm{inside}(\mathrm{now}, T)$
	$\neg\,\mathrm{inside}(\mathrm{now}, T_{+1})$
	$T' = T_{+1}$

e	$I\ T\ T_{+1}\ T'\ n$
	$\mathrm{holds}(e, I)$
	$\mathrm{intPartOf}(I, T')$
	$\mathrm{intPartOf}(T', T_{+1})$
	$\mathrm{calInt}(T, n, \text{*Week*}, c)$
	$\mathrm{calInt}(T_{+1}, n+1, \text{*Week*}, c)$
	$\mathrm{inside}(\mathrm{now}, T)$
	$\neg\,\mathrm{inside}(\mathrm{now}, T_{+1})$
	$\mathrm{Thursday}(T')$

The most interesting difference between next day and next Thursday therefore is that in the former case the minimal interval that contains now and a day is of unit length *Day*, while in the latter case the minimal interval that contains now and a Thursday is of unit length *Week*.

Now we could give an interpretation for last along the same lines, assuming that last D refers to that calendar or clock interval T' of type D such that T is the smallest calendar or clock interval that contains both now and an interval of type D, and T_{-1} is the calendar or clock interval that precedes T.

Exercise 8.3   Show that given the above semantics for next, next day is equivalent to tomorrow.

Exercise 8.4   Specify the semantics of last and of January, and compose both to the semantics of last January.

Exercise 8.5   Specify the semantics of this and show that it yields an appropriate semantics for this week.

Exercise 8.6   Specify syntactic and semantic representations for in *n* days and *n* days ago.

8.3   FURTHER READING

The time interval calculus goes back to Allen and Ferguson [1994]. Other calculi for reasoning about time, events and states are the *event calculus* [Shanahan, 1999] and the *situation calculus* [Reiter, 1991]. A linguistic temporal ontology was developed by [Moens and Steedman, 1988]. Formal treatments of tense and aspect in linguistics can be found for example in Steedman [1995] and Kamp and Reyle [1993]. Annotation of temporal events has received quite some consideration recently (see UzZaman and Allen [2010] and Pustejovsky et al. [2005]) and a standard for this, TimeML [Pustejovsky et al., 2010], has been developed. The relation between the time ontology of Hobbs and Pan and TimeML has been discussed by Hobbs and Pustejovsky [2003]. A formal approach to interpretation of natural language based on the event calculus has been presented by Lambalgen and Hamm [2005].

Ontology-Based Interpretation for Question Answering

Having started from ontologies as formal representations of a domain conceptualization, we constructed lexica enriching them with linguistic information and from those lexica automatically generated grammars. We have then walked through the whole interpretation process, combining meaning representations of words and phrases into meaning representations of whole sentences. We have further shown how we can deal with ambiguities exploiting ontological reasoning and we have discussed aspects related to the interpretation of temporal expressions. Finally it is time to integrate all of this in a real-world application, the icing on our cake: question answering.

First, we will define the task of question answering, in particular over structured knowledge sources, turning to the specific case of RDF data and its corresponding query language, SPARQL. In the main part of the chapter we will then show how we can extend the interpretation process that we have built up so far to transform natural language questions into formal queries which can be used to retrieve answers from a data repository. Last but not least we will give an outlook on what is needed to scale our approach to the huge, wild web of data out there.

9.1 QUESTION ANSWERING OVER STRUCTURED DATA

Question answering is the task of automatically retrieving answers to natural language questions—in the context of the soccer domain questions such as the following ones:

141.   (a) Which was the first team to win the world championship?

     (b) Give me all current Swedish national players.

     (c) How many hexagons are on a soccer ball?

     (d) Did Pelé ever miss a penalty kick?

Achieving this requires two major components. First, of course, we need a way to understand the information need that is expressed. Since we have just spent a whole book on the automatic interpretation of natural language, we are ready to go. And second, we need an interface to some kind of knowledge base that contains the answer. Sources for question answering are twofold. Traditionally, there has been a strong focus on question answering from unstructured data, extracting answers to questions in natural language from newspaper articles, websites, etc. Already in the late 1960s and early 1970s, people also started working on structured data, especially on answering information needs with respect to databases [Androutsopoulos et al., 1995]. When turning to structured data, the task of question answering is the following:

> For a given natural language question, construct a formal query that retrieves the answers from a data repository.

More recently, data on the Semantic Web has attracted growing interest. As there is more and more RDF data being published,[1] there is a growing need for intuitive, human-friendly ways of accessing this data—especially ways that hide the specific data formats from everyday users and allow them to express their information need in natural language, using their own terms. The main task of a question answering system then is to construct a formal query from natural language input. The standard querying language for RDF data, recommended by the World Wide Web Consortium, is SPARQL (*SPARQL Protocol and RDF Query Language*).[2] We will introduce its basics in the next section.

Before doing so, let us briefly look at an example, to get a taste of the task and also highlight some of the challenges involved. Consider the arguably quite easy question in 142a. The SPARQL query that expresses this information need with respect to our soccer ontology would look as the one in 142b. It says: Give me all instantiations of t, such that there is some r that is of type `PlayerRole` and that is related to `GianluigiBuffon` by means of the property `player` and to t by means of the property `team`. Executed on a comprehensive dataset, this query would retrieve the answers in 142c.

142. (a) Which teams did Buffon play for?

(b)
```
SELECT ?t WHERE {
    ?r a soccer:PlayerRole .
    ?r soccer:player soccer:GianluigiBuffon .
    ?r soccer:team ?t .
}
```

(c) `soccer:Parma, soccer:Juventus`

We can already identify two major challenges when constructing queries from natural language questions. The first one consists of bridging the *lexical gap*, i.e., the gap between natural language expressions and ontology labels. In the case of player names this is usually straightforward. For example, the name Buffon refers to the ontology individual `GianluigiBuffon`. For classes and especially properties, the correspondence is often less straightforward. For instance, there are different ways for verbalizing the class `Match`, either as match or game. In our case, the question contains the verb play for, but there is no ontology property that has a similar label. Even worse, the concept of playing for some team is expressed by the complex construct of being related to a player role (or maybe even more specifically a goalkeeper role) that is related to the team in

---

[1]For the current state of the so-called *Linked Open Data cloud*, see `http://lod-cloud.net/state/`.
[2]`http://www.w3.org/TR/rdf-sparql-query/`

question, i.e., in lines 3–5 in the above query in 142b. This constitutes the second major challenge: bridging the *structural gap*, i.e., the gap between the semantic structure of the natural language question and the structure of the underlying conceptualization. In the course of this book we have actually seen a lot of examples where there is a clear mismatch between the conceptualization of the soccer domain and the way we talk about it in natural language. We have also discussed how to tackle this. In fact, our whole grammar generation and interpretation process is built on the idea of a lexicon-ontology interface, i.e., a way to align ontology concepts and natural language expressions.

Exercise 9.1 Which semantic representation would our interpretation process build for the question in 142a? Check how close it is to the query in 142b.

9.2 QUERYING STRUCTURED DATA

Information on the Semantic Web is most commonly represented in RDF (for refreshing your RDF, see Section 1.4). The information that Pelé played for the Brazilian soccer club Santos FC, for example, is represented by the following triple in DBpedia:

143. ```
PREFIX dbpedia: <http://dbpedia.org/ontology/>
PREFIX resource: <http://dbpedia.org/resource/>

resource:Pelé dbpedia:team resource:Santos_FC .
```

The standard language for querying RDF is SPARQL. A basic SPARQL query consists of a SELECT part that specifies which variable instantiations should be returned, and a WHERE part, the body of the query, which specifies *graph patterns* that can be seen as conditions that any binding of the query variables should fulfill. A very simple graph pattern is a set of RDF triples in Turtle syntax, possibly using variables, which are prefixed with either $ or ?. A simple query for selecting the teams that Pelé played for is the following:

144. ```
PREFIX dbpedia:  <http://dbpedia.org/ontology/>
PREFIX resource: <http://dbpedia.org/resource/>

SELECT ?x WHERE {
  resource:Pelé dbpedia:team ?x .
}
```

This query will return all instantiations of the variable x such that the data contains the graph specified in the body of the query, in this case simply the triple resource:Pelé dbpedia:team x, for every instantiation x. One such instantiation is http://dbpedia.org/resource/Santos_FC.

We will see more complex SPARQL queries in the course of the chapter, introducing additional constructs whenever we need them. At this point we will consider just one more example, demonstrating ASK queries and aggregation operations. Take the question in 145a. The corresponding query is very similar to the one in 142b above, but answering it involves not listing but counting the teams that Cruyff played for. To this end, we use the aggregation operation COUNT. The query is given in 145b. Additionally, we prefix the variable t in the SELECT part with the modifier DISTINCT in order to count only different teams. This is important, as Cruyff played for Ajax Amsterdam twice in his career, so there will be two player roles connecting them.

145. (a) For how many teams did Johan Cruyff play?

(b) PREFIX soccer: <http://www.ontosem.net/ontologies/soccer#>

```
SELECT COUNT(DISTINCT ?t) WHERE {
  ?r a soccer:PlayerRole .
  ?r soccer:player soccer:JohanCruyff .
  ?r soccer:team ?t .
}
```

A similar question is the one in 146a, formulated with respect to DBpedia. However, in this case we are not looking for variable instantiations but simply for a yes or no answer. The corresponding query with respect to DBpedia, given in 146b, therefore uses ASK instead of SELECT. An ASK query returns true if the graph pattern specified in the body of the query has some instantiation, and false otherwise. Moreover, we use a FILTER construct that filters the graph patterns and selects only those where the number g of goals is greater than 30.

146. (a) Did Cruyff score more than 30 goals when playing for the national team?

(b) PREFIX dbpedia: <http://dbpedia.org/property/>
    PREFIX resource: <http://dbpedia.org/resource/>

```
ASK WHERE {
  resource:Johan_Cruyff dbpedia:nationalgoals ?g .
  FILTER (?g > 30)
}
```

Note that in this case the mismatch between natural language and data is especially big, as the property nationalgoals is expressed as score...when playing for the national team.

Exercise 9.2   Build a SPARQL query for the question Did George Best score more goals for the national team than Cruyff? Send it to the DBpedia SPARQL endpoint at *http://dbpedia.org/sparql/* and check what the answer is.

Exercise 9.3   How would the query in 146b look with respect to our soccer ontology? (Extend the ontology if necessary.)

9.3   FROM NATURAL LANGUAGE QUESTIONS TO ANSWERS

Recall the overall architecture of ontology-based interpretation that we gave in Figure 1.1. Figure 9.1 depicts that architecture again and now extends it with an interface between users, expressing their information need in natural language, and a data repository. That is, we want to construct a system that gets a natural language question from a user as input, sends this question to the interpretation component, computes a semantic representation and transforms it into a query which can then be sent to a data repository that returns the result to be passed on to the user, possibly rendered as natural language answer.

Figure 9.2 shows the architecture of the interpretation component as we developed it in the previous chapters. Input is now a natural language question. On the basis of a grammar that was automatically generated from an ontology lexicon (and thus is aligned to an underlying domain

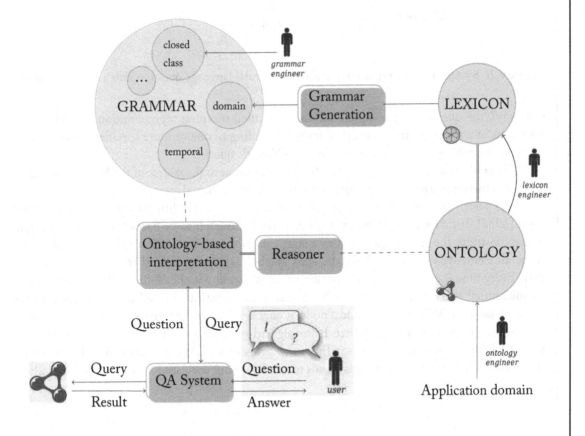

Figure 9.1: Approach to the ontology-based interpretation of natural language as back-end for a question answering system.

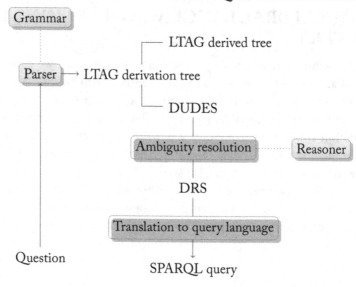

Figure 9.2: System architecture for transforming a natural language question into a SPARQL query.

ontology), the question is parsed and an underspecified meaning representation is constructed. By means of a reasoner, ambiguities are resolved, leading to one or more specified meaning representations, which are then translated into a SPARQL query.

The only two components that we did not yet look at in the course of the book is the parser and the transformation of a meaning representation into a formal query.

As parser, we use an Earley-type parser based on the algorithm proposed by Schabes and Joshi [1988]. It first selects all trees with leaf nodes that match some part of the input question. These constitute the search space. Given a start category, e.g., S or DP, it picks from the search space all elementary trees that have the start symbol as root node, and traverses them depth-first. Every time it encounters a substitution node, it checks whether some of the other trees can be substituted there, and if so, proceeds traversing the substituted tree before returning to the substitution node. When it meets a leaf node, it checks whether the term corresponds to the term that is to be read from the input next. If the algorithm manages to traverse the whole tree that way, it has successfully found a parse. This parse gives us a LTAG derivation tree. For instance, the question Which match had no goals? leads to the following derivation tree (see Section 3.2):

147.

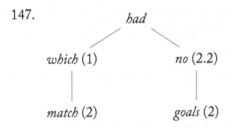

Next, syntactic and semantic composition rules apply in tandem in order to construct a LTAG derived tree and a DUDES:

148.

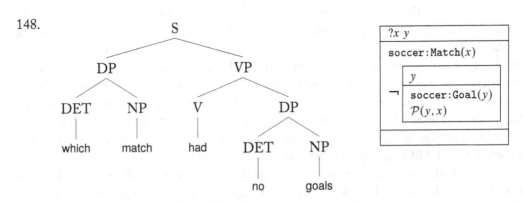

Note that the variable x is marked with a question mark in order to indicate that this is a query variable that needs to be bound to a particular value in an answer to the query. In order to achieve this, we assume that the meaning representations of wh-forms, such as which, who, what, etc., introduce a marked discourse referent, e.g., $?x$, while all other determiners introduce unmarked ones, as before. Also note that the DUDES contains a metavariable $\mathcal{P}$ without any instantiation pairs. This stems from the interpretation of the verb had, which denotes an underspecified relation. The next step consists in the disambiguation procedure searching the ontology for a property connecting goals and matches, which resolves $\mathcal{P}$ to the property inMatch, finally yielding the following specified DRS:

149.

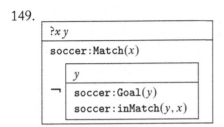

The final step consists in translating this DRS into a SPARQL query. To this end, we follow some simple transformation rules:

- All marked discourse referents are collected and added to the SELECT part of the query. If there are no marked referents, the query will be an ASK query; this will be the case for yes/no questions, such as Did Holland ever win the World Cup?

- All unary predicates, such as soccer:Team(x) are translated into rdf:type statements, such as ?x rdf:type soccer:Team .

- All binary predicates, such as soccer:leadsTo(x, y), are translated into triples, such as ?x soccer:leadsTo ?y .

A bit more consideration is required for translating quantifier structures and negation.

First, the quantifiers every and all can usually be discarded, because a query returns all instantiations of a variable anyway. Exceptions are expressions like the team that won all games. There is no direct way to express this in SPARQL. Answering such information needs would require a query engine that is able to construct subqueries and evaluate them in the correct order, e.g., first retrieving all games and then retrieving the teams that stand in the winner relation with those games. Also the quantifiers some and a(n) have no direct correspondent in SPARQL. We could implement some of these quantifiers using procedural elements, such as the ability to limit the number of results by means of the solution modifier LIMIT or by sampling from the answers returned by the SPARQL query. However, we do not discuss this further here.

What about more than two or less than ten? The DP more than two x, for example, introduces a variable x, which needs to be counted if it is the argument of an object property, thus yielding COUNT(?x), or simply be returned as ?x in case it is the numeral value of a datatype property. Next, the answers should be filtered with respect to the resulting number, either by means of a filter, such as FILTER (?x > 2), or by means of a HAVING construct, such as HAVING (COUNT(?x) > 2). The latter is necessary as filter expressions are not allowed to contain aggregation functions like COUNT. Here are examples for both cases (leaving out the prefix definitions):

150.   (a) Which stadium has more than 30,000 seats?

    (b)
```
SELECT ?x WHERE {
    ?x a soccer:Stadium .
    ?x soccer:capacity ?y .
    FILTER (?y > 30 000)
}
```

151.   (a) Which team won more than two games?

    (b)
```
SELECT ?x WHERE {
    ?x a soccer:Team .
    ?y a soccer:Match.
    ?y soccer:winner ?x .
}
GROUP BY ?x HAVING (COUNT(?y) > 2)
```

Exercise 9.4   What would happen if the query in 150b would have specified GROUP BY ?x HAVING (COUNT(?y) > 30,000) instead of using the filter?

Exercise 9.5   Think about how the ambiguity representation and resolution mechanism from Chapter 7 can be adapted in order to account for the ambiguity that, in the case of object properties, variable instantiations need to be counted, while, in the case of datatype properties, the variable value has to be processed without counting.

Another special case is the quantifier the most. Consider the question Which team won the most games? Answering it requires the following procedure: For each team count the games that it won, and then determine the team with the maximum number of such games. We have already seen how to count; we can determine the maximum number of something by first ordering the results in descending order (or ascending if we are interested in the minimum number) and then pick only the first result. Here is an example:

152.   (a) Which stadium has the most seats?

   (b) ```
SELECT ?x WHERE {
    ?x a soccer:Stadium .
    ?x soccer:capacity ?y .
}
ORDER BY DESC(?y)
LIMIT 1
```

153.   (a)  Which team won the most games?

   (b)  ```
SELECT ?x WHERE {
    ?x a soccer:Team .
    ?y a soccer:Match.
    ?y soccer:winner ?x .
}
ORDER BY DESC(COUNT(?x))
LIMIT 1
```

The query in 153b actually only works in SPARQL 1.1., as in earlier versions it is not allowed to aggregate in an ORDER BY clause. In that case you would need to add COUNT(?x) AS ?n to the SELECT clause and then order by ?n.

This covers the most common quantifiers. Of the ones we have encountered in the course of the book, no is the only one left. There are only very limited possibilities for expressing negation in SPARQL; the most prominent one is by means of a filter that requires variables to be unbound, as in the following example.

154.   (a) Which matches had no goals?

```
(b) SELECT ?x WHERE {
        ?x a soccer:Match .
        ?y a soccer:Goal .
        ?y soccer:inMatch ?x .
        FILTER !BOUND(?y)
    }
```

Here BOUND(?y) checks whether there is an instantiation of ?y, and ! is a negation operator. The quantifier no is thus implemented in a negation-by-failure fashion like, for example, in Prolog systems.

Exercise 9.6   Build a meaning representation for the following questions and sentences and transform it into a SPARQL query according to the above rules.

155.   (a) Give me all teams that won no game and no tournament.

   (b) Which team does the player with the most red cards play for?

   (c) Which player never missed a penalty kick?

9.4   IMPLEMENTATION

The system depicted in Figure 9.2 builds on components that we have been looking at throughout the book as well as on a parser and an algorithm for transforming a DRS into a SPARQL query described in the previous section. We have implemented exactly this architecture in a question answering system called *Pythia* [Unger and Cimiano, 2011b]. A pointer to the code and a demo can be found on the book website.

9.5   FURTHER READING

Recently there has been an increasing interest in question answering over Semantic Web data. For an overview of state-of-the-art systems see Lopez et al. [2011]. A system that does not rely on grammars but uses a linguistic component very close to the one presented in this chapter is TBSL [Unger et al., 2012], a template-based approach to the construction of SPARQL queries. Some of the interest in developing Semantic Web question answering systems has been stirred by the open challenges on Question Answering over Linked Data (QALD) [Lopez et al., 2013], which provide datasets together with gold-standard questions and queries for benchmarking purposes.

CHAPTER 10

Conclusion

We have presented an ontology-based approach to natural language interpretation that puts the ontology at the center of the interpretation process. The role of the ontology is to define the scope of what needs to be interpreted, both in terms of conceptual granularity as well as linguistic coverage. Such an ontology-centric approach allows us to channel efforts of lexicon creation to those aspects that are relevant to a given domain and ontology and thus provides a scope to lexicon engineering, knowledge modeling and knowledge capture activities. This book is the only one that presents a principled approach to compositional semantics with respect to Semantic Web ontologies and representation formalisms such as OWL, RDF(S) and SPARQL.

The approach we have presented is principled in the sense that the interpretation process generates only interpretations that are compatible with the ontology (in terms of corresponding to some element in the ontology) and that are aligned to the ontology (in the sense of sharing the semantic vocabulary). In fact, from the point of view of an application that builds on a given ontology, any semantic representation that is not aligned to the ontology is useless as it could not be processed further by the backend system or application in a meaningful way.

Moreover, our approach emphasizes three important aspects: modularity, use of standards, and formalism-independence.

Our approach is modular in at least two ways. First, the ontology or set of ontologies as well as the ontology lexica that the system exploits for the interpretation of natural language can be exchanged straightforwardly at any time, adapting the behavior of the system and the semantic representations it generates to a particular domain or set of domains. As the grammars are automatically generated from the underlying ontology-lexicon, exchanging the ontology and the corresponding lexicon will also lead to different grammars. Further, all reasoning the system performs is done through an OWL reasoner accessed through corresponding APIs. Thus if the ontology is changed, the actual interpretation component will not even take notice of it as it will simply use the same interface to communicate with the reasoner. Moreover, our approach is modular in the sense that the resources the system uses to guide interpretation can be constructed and maintained independently of each other. For example, for each ontology that the system uses for interpretation, there might be one or more ontology lexica that are developed independently of each other. Such a modular approach fosters a *divide and conquer* paradigm that makes it easier to develop and maintain the resources needed as the effort can be distributed among different groups of people with complementary skills and varying levels of expertise.

We have outlined an approach that makes consistent use of open standards, in particular for knowledge modeling (the web ontology language OWL) and data representation (RDF). Building on open standards is in our view key to foster the reuse of resources beyond the applications that particular systems have been designed for. In the same vein, we have proposed a declarative formalism for the representation of ontology lexica, *lemon*. One of the advantages of *lemon* is its theory- and formalism-neutrality. In fact, *lemon* lexica are not committed to any particular linguistic theory or formalism. This also facilitates their exploitation because grammars in any formalism of our choice can be generated automatically. In this sense, the lexica become a true asset of their developers and the community, independently of any particular formalisms and theories. This again facilitates the reuse of resources.

The current mainstream in computational linguistics unfortunately regards an ontology-compliant representation only as an afterthought, concentrating on the generation of semantic representations of natural language that are independent of a particular domain and the conceptual design decisions that the developer of a system makes. In sum, it would generate the same semantic representations independently of the domain and ontology in question. We think that this is wrong. The semantic and conceptual distinctions clearly vary between domains and applications, as does for example the number and granularity of meanings of a particular word. One representation that is the same regardless of domains and applications does not do justice to this. Further, a representation that is domain-independent makes it difficult to connect it to a given ontology to allow for domain-specific inferences. The exploitation of an ontology to guide the interpretation process represents a principled design choice. In fact, as our examples in this book have shown, without suitable background knowledge, only the surface meaning of a sentence can be captured, while the actual important aspects which follow from it would remain hidden and inaccessible. Interpretation that matters requires an ontology to guide the process of interpretation, perform relevant inferences and thus restrict the interpretation to models that are actually possible given the commitment of the ontological theory.

Overall, there are not many NLP approaches to semantic interpretation of natural language that exploit ontologies in a principled fashion, e.g., for inferencing and disambiguation. However, if no principled approaches are available to exploit richly axiomatized domain ontologies for interpretation of natural language, this might also explain why not many richly axiomatized domain ontologies that could be exploited by NLP systems have been created so far. Any approach that aims at deeper interpretation of natural language beyond mirroring syntactic dependencies only will definitely require a representation that is aligned to the ontology and thus can be used to constrain the possible interpretations of a sentence in context.

Clearly, the instantiation of our approach that we have presented in this book lacks robustness and coverage of linguistic phenomena. However, this is not a deficiency of our approach itself, but of the particular implementation which relies on deterministic parsers, perfect reasoning, and so on. Robustness can be incorporated by using machine learning techniques that compute for instance the most likely interpretation of a given natural language sentence. Future work will be devoted to developing statistical approaches trained on the basis of ontology-aligned semantic representations. Thus, our proposed framework does not exclude statistical approaches to NLP; in fact, it will require such techniques to get the necessary robustness and scalability.

There is also a long-term vision behind our approach. We envision an ecosystem of ontologies and connected lexica, that become available and accessible over the web based on open standards and protocols. Such an ecosystem facilitates the task of finding a suitable ontology in addition to one or several ontology lexica expressing how the properties and classes in this ontology are verbalized in different languages. If ontologies and associated lexica are available over the web, somebody wanting to build an NLP application can find and download them, generate grammars automatically, add some domain-independent ontologies with their lexica and build a new ontology- and domain-specific NLP system ideally by reusing existing building blocks and components. Leveraging the web and the open web standards in order to create a web-based ecosystem of lexical, linguistic and domain-specific ontological resources that are linked to each other might in fact become a key aspect toward increasing the adoption of NLP technologies and creating incentives for the development of high-quality knowledge resources that can be exploited by NLP systems that are part of and consume data from this ecosystem.

Bibliography

Nabil Abdullah and Richard A. Frost. Adjectives: A uniform semantic approach. In *Proceedings of the 18th Conference of the Canadian Society for Computational Studies of Intelligence*, pages 330–341, 2005. DOI: 10.1007/11424918_35. 75

Anne Abeillé, Marie-Hélène Candito, and Alexandra Kinyon. FTAG: current status and parsing scheme. In *Proceedings of Venezia per il Trattamento Automatico delle Lingue (VExTAL'99)*, pages 283–292, 1999. 94

James F. Allen. Towards a general theory of action and time. *Artificial Intelligence*, 23:123–154, 1984. DOI: 10.1016/0004-3702(84)90008-0. 119

James F. Allen and George Ferguson. Actions and events in interval temporal logic. *Journal of Logic and Computation*, 4(5):531–579, 1994. DOI: 10.1093/logcom/4.5.531. 129

James F. Allen and George Ferguson. Actions and events in interval temporal logic. In Oliviero Stock, editor, *Spatial and Temporal Reasoning*, pages 205–245. Kluwer, 1997. DOI: 10.1007/978-0-585-28322-7. 119

Ion Androutsopoulos, Graeme D. Ritchie, and Peter Thanisch. Natural language interfaces to databases: An introduction. *Natural Language Engineering*, 1(1):29–81, 1995. DOI: 10.1017/S135132490000005X. 132

Franz Baader, Diego Calvanese, Deborah L. McGuinness, Daniele Nardi, and Peter F. Patel-Schneider, editors. *The description logic handbook: theory, implementation, and applications*. Cambridge University Press, 2003. 32

Marco Baroni, Raffaella Bernardi, and Roberto Zamparelli. Frege in space: A program for compositional distributional semantics. *Linguistic Issues in Language Technology*, to appear. 7

David Beckett and Tim Berners-Lee. Turtle—Terse RDF Triple Language. W3C Team Submission, W3C, 2011. http://www.w3.org/TeamSubmission/turtle/. 11

Tim Berners-Lee, James Hendler, and Ora Lassila. The semantic web. *Scientific American*, 284 (5):34–43, 2001. DOI: 10.1038/scientificamerican0501-34. 9

Steven Bird and Mark Liberman. A formal framework for linguistic annotation. *Speech Communication*, 33(1):23–60, 2001. DOI: 10.1016/S0167-6393(00)00068-6. 10

Patrick Blackburn and Johan Bos. *Representation and Inference for Natural Language: A First Course in Computational Semantics*. CSLI Press, 2005. 57

Johan Bos. Predicate logic unplugged. In *Proceedings of the 10th Amsterdam Colloquium*, pages 133–142, 1995. 115

Pierrette Bouillon and Evelyne Viegas. The description of adjectives for natural language processing: Theoretical and applied perspectives. In *Proceedings of Traitement Automatique des Langues Naturelles (TALN)*, 1999. 75

Harry Bunt. Underspecification in semantic representations: Which technique for what purpose? In *Proceedings of the 5th International Workshop on Computational Semantics (IWCS)*, pages 37–54, 1995. DOI: 10.1007/978-1-4020-5958-2_4. 115

Jean Carletta, Stefan Evert, Ulrich Heid, and Jonathan Kilgour. The NITE XML toolkit: data model and query. *Language Resources and Evaluation*, 39(4):313–334, 2005. DOI: 10.1007/s10579-006-9001-9. 10

Rudolf Carnap. *Meaning and Necessity*. University of Chicago Press, 1947. 7

Christian Chiarcos, Sebastian Hellmann, Sebastian Nordhoff, Steven Moran, Richard Littauer, Judith Eckle-Kohler, Iryna Gurevych, Silvana Hartmann, Michael Matuschek, and Christian M. Meyer. The open linguistics working group. In *Proceedings of the 8th International Conference on Language Resources and Evaluation (LREC)*, 2012. 66

Christian Chiarcos, John McCrae, Philipp Cimiano, and Christiane Fellbaum. Towards open data for linguistics: Linguistic linked data. In Alessandro Oltramari, Piek Vossen, Lu Qin, and Eduard Hovy, editors, *New Trends of Research in Ontologies and Lexical Resources*. Springer, 2013. DOI: 10.1007/978-3-642-31782-8. 10

Philipp Cimiano and Uwe Reyle. Ontology-based semantic construction, underspecification and disambiguation. In *Proceedings of the Lorraine/Saarland Workshop on Prospects and Recent Advances in the Syntax-Semantics Interface*, pages 33–38, 2003. 115

Philipp Cimiano. *Ontology learning and population from text: algorithms, evaluation and applications*. Springer, 2006. 6

Philipp Cimiano. Flexible semantic composition with DUDES. In *Proceedings of the 8th International Conference on Computational Semantics (IWCS)*, 2009. 47, 57

Philipp Cimiano, Anette Frank, and Uwe Reyle. UDRT-based semantics construction for LTAG—and what it tells us about the role of adjunction in LTAG. In *Proceedings of the 7th International Workshop on Computational Semantics (IWCS)*, pages 41–52, 2007. 57

Philipp Cimiano, Paul Buitelaar, John McCrae, and Michael Sintek. LexInfo: A declarative model for the lexicon-ontology interface. *Journal of Web Semantics: Science, Services and Agents on the World Wide Web*, 9(1):29–51, 2011. DOI: 10.1016/j.websem.2010.11.001. 79

Philipp Cimiano, John McCrae, Paul Buitelaar, and Elena Montiel-Ponsoda. On the role of senses in the ontology-lexicon. In Alessandro Oltramari, Piek Vossen, Lu Qin, and Eduard Hovy, editors, *New Trends of Research in Ontologies and Lexical Resources*, Theory and Applications of Natural Language Processing, pages 43–62. Springer, 2013. DOI: 10.1007/978-3-642-31782-8. 3, 79

Guglielmo Cinque. *Adverbs and functional heads: A cross-linguistic perspective.* Oxford University Press, 1999. 67

Ann Copestake, Dan Flickinger, Ivan A. Sag, and Carl Pollard. Minimal Recursion Semantics: An introduction. *Research on Language and Computation*, 3:281–332, 2005. DOI: 10.1007/s11168-006-6327-9. 57, 115

Benoît Crabbé, Denys Duchier, Claire Gardent, Joseph Le Roux, and Yannick Parmentier. XMG : eXtensible MetaGrammar. *Computational Linguistics*, 39(3):1–66, 2013. DOI: 10.1162/COLI_a_00144. 94

James R. Curran, Stephen Clark, and Johan Bos. Linguistically motivated large-scale NLP with C&C and Boxer. In *Proceedings of the 45th Annual Meeting of the Association for Computational Linguistics (ACL)*, 2007. 7

Ido Dagan, Bill Dolan, Bernado Magnini, and Dan Roth. Recognizing textual entailment: Rational, evaluation and approaches. *Natural Language Engineering*, 15(4):i–xvii, 2009. DOI: 10.1017/S1351324909990209. 6

Paul Dekker. Existential disclosure. *Linguistics and Philosophy*, 16(6):561–587, 1993. DOI: 10.1007/BF00985434. 79

Paul Dekker. A guide to dynamic semantics. In Klaus von Heusinger, Claudia Maienborn, and Paul Portner, editors, *Semantics: An international handbook of natural language meaning*, volume 1, pages 923–945. De Gruyter Mouton, 2011. 42, 57

Jos de Bruin and Remko Scha. The interpretation of relational nouns. In *Proceedings of the 26th Annual Meeting of the Association for Computational Linguistics (ACL)*, pages 25–32, 1988. DOI: 10.3115/982023.982027. 69, 79

Katrin Erk. Vector space models of word meaning and phrase meaning: A survey. *Language and Linguistics Compass*, 6(10):635–653, 2012. DOI: 10.1002/lnco.362. 7

Mariano Fernández-Lopez, Asunción Gómez-Pérez, and Natalia Juristo. METHONTOL-OGY: from ontological art towards ontological engineering. In *Proceedings of the AAAI Spring Symposium Series on Ontological Engineering*, pages 33–40, 1997. 32

Robert Frank. *Phrase structure composition and syntactic dependencies*, volume 38 of *Current Studies in Linguistics*. MIT Press, 2002. 34, 35

William Frawley. *Linguistic Semantics*. Erlbaum, 1992. 75

Eduardo H. Galeano. *Soccer in Sun and Shadow*. Verso, 2003. 16

L.T.F. Gamut. *Logic, language and meaning. Volume 1: Introduction to logic*. University of Chicago Press, 1991. xvi

Aldo Gangemi and Valentina Presutti. Ontology design patterns. In Stefan Staab and Rudi Studer, editors, *Handbook on Ontologies*, International Handbooks on Information Systems, pages 221–243. Springer, 2009. DOI: 10.1007/978-3-540-92673-3. 70

Claire Gardent and Laura Kallmeyer. Semantic construction in feature-based TAG. In *Proceedings of the 10th Conference of the European Chapter of the Association for Computational Linguistics (EACL)*, 2003. DOI: 10.3115/1067807.1067825. 57

Ruifang Ge and Raymond J. Mooney. Discriminative reranking for semantic parsing. In *Proceedings of the 21st International Conference on Computational Linguistics and 44th Annual Meeting of the Association for Computational Linguistics (ACL)*, 2006. 7

Michael Genesereth and Eric Kao. *Introduction to Logic*. Synthesis Lectures on Computer Science. Morgan & Claypool Publishers, 2013. DOI: 10.2200/s00518ed2v01y201306csl006. xvi

Gregory Grefenstette. Sextant: Exploring unexplored contexts for semantic extraction from syntactic analysis. In *Proceedings of the 30th Annual Meeting of the Association for Computational Linguistics (ACL)*, pages 324–326, 1992. DOI: 10.3115/981967.982020. 7

Thomas R. Gruber. Toward principles for the design of ontologies used for knowledge sharing. In *Formal Analysis in Conceptual Analysis and Knowledge Representation*. Kluwer, 1993. DOI: 10.1006/ijhc.1995.1081. 17

Nicola Guarino and Pierdaniele Giaretta. Ontologies and knowledge bases: Towards a terminological clarification. In Nicolaas J. Mars, editor, *Towards Very Large Knowledge Bases: Knowledge Building and Knowledge Sharing*, pages 25–32. IOS Press, 1995. 17

Nicola Guarino. Understanding, building and using ontologies. *International Journal of Human-Computer Studies*, 46(2):293–310, 1997. DOI: 10.1006/ijhc.1996.0091. 17

Nicola Guarino. Some ontological principles for designing upper level lexical resources. In *Proceedings of First International Conference on Language Resources and Evaluation (LREC)*, pages 527–534, 1998. 17, 31

Nicola Guarino and Christopher Welty. A formal ontology of properties. In *Proceedings of the 12th European Workshop on Knowledge Acquisition, Modeling and Management*, pages 97–112, 2000. DOI: 10.1007/3-540-39967-4_8. 31

Nicola Guarino and Christopher Welty. An overview of OntoClean. In Stefan Staab and Rudi Studer, editors, *Handbook on Ontologies*, pages 151–159. Springer, 2004. DOI: 10.1007/978-3-540-24750-0. 17, 31

Chung-hye Han, Juntae Yoon, Nari Kim, and Martha Palmer. A Feature-Based Lexicalized Tree Adjoining Grammar for Korean. Technical Report IRCS-00-04, University of Pennsylvania, 2000. 94

Amac Herdagdelen, Katrin Erk, and Marco Baroni. Measuring semantic relatedness with vector space models and random walks. In *Proceedings of the Workshop on Graph-based Methods for Natural Language Processing*, pages 50–53, 2009. 7

Donald Hindle and Mats Rooth. Structural ambiguity and lexical relations. *Computational Linguistics*, 19(1):103–120, 1993. 116

Graeme Hirst. *Semantic interpretation and the resolution of ambiguity*. Cambridge University Press, 1987. DOI: 10.1017/CBO9780511554346. 116

Pascal Hitzler, Markus Krötzsch, and Sebastian Rudolph. *Foundations of Semantic Web Technologies*. Chapman & Hall/CRC, 2009. 28, 29, 32

Jerry R. Hobbs and James Pustejovsky. Annotating and reasoning about time and events. In *Proceedings of the AAAI Spring Symposium on Logical Formalization of Commonsense Reasoning*, pages 1292–1298, 2003. 129

Jerry R. Hobbs and Feng Pan. An ontology of time for the semantic web. *ACM Transactions on Asian Language Information Processing*, 3(1):66–85, 2004. DOI: 10.1145/1017068.1017073. 117, 118, 119

Jerry R. Hobbs, Mark E. Stickel, Douglas E. Appelt, and Paul A. Martin. Interpretation as abduction. *Artificial Intelligence*, 63(1–2):69–142, 1993. DOI: 10.1016/0004-3702(93)90015-4. 115

Wilfrid Hodges. *Logic: An introduction to elementary logic*. Penguin books, second edition, 2001. xvi

Nancy Ide and Jean Véronis. Introduction to the special issue on word sense disambiguation: the state of the art. *Computational Linguistics*, 24(1):2–40, 1998. 115

Aravind K. Joshi. How much context-sensitivity is necessary for characterizing structural descriptions-tree adjoining grammars. In David Dowty, Lauri Karttunen, and Arnold Zwicky, editors, *Natural Language Processing: Theoretical, Computational and Psychological Perspectives*. Cambridge University Press, 1985. DOI: 10.1017/CBO9780511597855. 34, 57

Aravind K. Joshi and Yves Schabes. Tree-adjoining grammars and lexicalized grammars. Technical report, University of Pennsylvania, 1991. 57

Aravind K. Joshi, Leon S. Levy, and Masako Takahashi. Tree adjunct grammars. *Journal of Computer and System Sciences*, 10(1):136–163, 1975. DOI: 10.1016/S0022-0000(75)80019-5. 34, 57

Laura Kallmeyer and Aravind K. Joshi. Factoring predicate argument and scope semantics: Underspecified semantics with LTAG. *Research on Language and Computation*, 1:3–58, 2003. DOI: 10.1023/A:1024564228892. 57

Laura Kallmeyer, Timm Lichte, Wolfgang Maier, Yannick Parmentier, and Johannes Dellert. Developing a TT-MCTAG for German with an RCG-based parser. In *Proceedings of the Sixth Language Resources and Evaluation Conference (LREC)*, pages 782–789, 2008. 94

Hans Kamp. A theory of truth and semantic representation. In Jeroen Groenendijk, Theo Janssen, and Martin Stokhof, editors, *Formal Methods in the Study of Language*, volume 135 of *Mathematical Centre Tracts*, pages 277–322. Mathematisch Centrum, 1981. 42

Hans Kamp and Uwe Reyle. *From Discourse to Logic. Introduction to Modeltheoretic Semantics of Natural Language, Formal Logic and Discourse Representation Theory*. Kluwer, 1993. 42, 57, 129

Hans Kamp, Josef van Genabith, and Uwe Reyle. Discourse representation theory. In Dov M. Gabbay and Franz Guenthner, editors, *Handbook of Philosophical Logic*, volume 15, pages 125–394. Springer, 2011. DOI: 10.1007/978-94-007-0485-5. 57

Ronald Kaplan and Joan Bresnan. Lexical-functional grammar: A formal system for grammatical representation. In Joan Bresnan, editor, *The mental representation of grammatical relations*. MIT Press, 1982. 57

Rohit J. Kate and Raymond J. Mooney. Using string-kernels for learning semantic parsers. In *Proceedings of the 21st International Conference on Computational Linguistics and 44th Annual Meeting of the Association for Computational Linguistics (ACL)*, 2006. DOI: 10.3115/1220175.1220290. 7

Marc Kemps-Snijders, Menzo Windhouwer, Peter Wittenburg, and Sue Ellen Wright. Isocat: Corralling data categories in the wild. In *Proceedings of the International Conference on Language Resources and Evaluation (LREC)*, pages 887–891, 2008. 65

Alexander Koller, Joachim Niehren, and Stefan Thater. Bridging the gap between underspecification formalisms: Hole semantics as dominance constraints. In *Proceedings of the 10th Conference of the European Chapter of the Association for Computational Linguistics (EACL)*, pages 195–202, 2003. 115

Michiel Van Lambalgen and Fritz Hamm, editors. *The proper treatment of events*. Blackwell Publishing, 2005. DOI: 10.1002/9780470759257. 129

Robert D. Levine and Detmar Meurers. Head-driven phrase structure grammar: Linguistic approach, formal foundations, and computational realization. In Keith Brown, editor, *Encyclopedia of Language and Linguistics*. Elsevier, 2nd edition, 2006. 57

Vanessa Lopez, Victoria Uren, Marta Sabou, and Enrico Motta. Is question answering fit for the semantic web? a survey. *Semantic Web Journal*, 2:125–155, 2011. DOI: 10.3233/SW-2011-0041. 140

Vanessa Lopez, Christina Unger, Philipp Cimiano, and Enrico Motta. Evaluating question answering over linked data. *Journal of Web Semantics*, 21(0), 2013. DOI: 10.1016/j.websem.2013.05.006. 140

Claudia Maienborn. Event semantics. In Claudia Maienborn, Klaus von Heusinger, and Paul Portner, editors, *Semantics: An international handbook of natural language meaning*, volume 1, pages 802–829. De Gruyter Mouton, 2011. 48

Chris Manning and Hinrich Schütze. *Foundations of Statistical Natural Language Processing*. MIT Press, 1999. 6

Frank Manola and Eric Miller. RDF Primer. W3C Recommendation, W3C, 2004. http://www.w3.org/TR/rdf-primer/. 9, 11

John McCrae and Christina Unger. Design patterns for engineering the ontology-lexicon interface. In Paul Buitelaar and Philipp Cimiano, editors, *Towards the Multilingual Semantic Web*. Springer, to appear. 80

John McCrae and Philipp Cimiano. Three steps for creating high-quality ontology lexica. In *Proceedings of the Workshop on Collaborative Resource Development and Delivery, collocated with the International Conference on Lexical Ressources and Evaluation (LREC)*, 2012. 79

John McCrae, Elena Montiel-Ponsoda, and Philipp Cimiano. Integrating WordNet and Wiktionary with lemon. *Linked Data in Linguistics*, pages 25–34, 2012a. DOI: 10.1007/978-3-642-28249-2_3. 65

John McCrae, Dennis Spohr, and Philipp Cimiano. Linking lexical resources and ontologies on the semantic web with lemon. In *Proceedings of the 8th Extended Semantic Web Conference (ESWC)*, pages 245–259. Springer, 2011. DOI: 10.1007/978-3-642-21034-1_17. 59, 79

John McCrae, Guadalupe Aguado-de Cea, Paul Buitelaar, Philipp Cimiano, Thierry Declerck, Asunción Gómez-Pérez, Jorge Gracia, Laura Hollink, Elena Montiel-Ponsoda, Dennis Spohr, and Tobias Wunner. Interchanging lexical resources on the semantic web. *Language Resources and Evaluation*, 46(4):701–719, 2012b. DOI: 10.1007/s10579-012-9182-3. 79

John McCrae, Elena Montiel-Ponsoda, and Philipp Cimiano. Collaborative semantic editing of linked data lexica. In *Proceedings of the International Conference on Language Resource and Evaluation (LREC)*, pages 2619–2625, 2012c. 79

Deborah L. McGuinness and Frank van Harmelen. OWL web ontology language overview. W3C Recommendation, W3C, 2004. http://www.w3.org/TR/owl-features/. 9

Jeff Mitchell and Mirella Lapata. Vector-based models of semantic composition. In *Proceedings of the 46th Annual Meeting of the Association for Computational Linguistics (ACL)*, pages 236–244, 2008. 7

Marc Moens and Mark Steedman. Temporal ontology and temporal reference. *Computational Linguistics*, 14(2):15–28, 1988. 129

Michael Moortgat. Categorial type logics. In Johan van Benthem and Alice ter Meulen, editors, *Handbook of Logic and Language*, pages 93–177. Elsevier, 1997. 57

Roberto Navigli. Word sense disambiguation: A survey. *ACM Computing Surveys*, 41(2):1–69, 2009. DOI: 10.1145/1459352.1459355. 6

Sergei Nirenburg and Viktor Raskin. *Ontological Semantics*. MIT Press, 2004. 4, 6, 79

Natalya F. Noy and Deborah L. McGuiness. Ontology development 101: A guide to creating your first ontology. Technical report, Stanford Medical Informatics, 2001. 17, 32

Daniel Oberle, Nicola Guarino, and Steffen Staab. What is an ontology? In Steffen Staab and Rudi Studer, editors, *Handbook of Ontologies*. Springer, 2nd edition, 2009. DOI: 10.1007/978-3-540-92673-3. 20, 21

Manfred Pinkal. Vagueness, Ambiguity, and Underspecification. In *Proceedings of Semantics and Linguistic Theory (SALT)*, pages 185–201, 1996. 116

Massimo Poesio and Uwe Reyle. Underspecification in anaphoric reference. In *Proceedings of the Fourth International Workshop on Computational Semantics (IWCS)*, 2001. 109

Paul Portner and Barbara Partee, editors. *Formal Semantics: The Essential Readings*. Blackwell, 2002. DOI: 10.1002/9780470758335. 57

Eric Prud'hommeaux and Andy Seaborne. SPARQL Query Language for RDF. W3C Recommendation, W3C, 2008. http://www.w3.org/TR/rdf-sparql-query/. 9

James Pustejovsky. The generative lexicon. *Computational Linguistics*, 17(4):409–441, 1991. 75

James Pustejovsky. The Semantics of Lexical Underspecification. *Folia Linguistica*, 32(3–4): 323–348, 2009. 116

James Pustejovsky, Robert Knippen, Jessica Littman, and Roser Sauri. Temporal and event information in natural language text. *Language Resources and Evaluation*, 39(2–3):123–164, 2005. DOI: 10.1007/s10579-005-7882-7. 129

James Pustejovsky, Kiyong Lee, Harry Bunt, and Laurent Romary. ISO-TimeML: An international standard for semantic annotation. In *Proceedings of the International Conference on Language Resources and Evaluation (LREC)*, 2010. 129

Aarne Ranta. *Grammatical Framework: Programming with Multilingual Grammars*. CSLI Publications, 2011. 57, 94

Victor Raskin and Sergei Nirenburg. Lexical semantics of adjectives. *Computing Research Laboratory, New Mexico State University*, 1995. 75, 77, 79

Raymond Reiter. The frame problem in the situation calculus: a simple solution (sometimes) and a completeness result for goal regression. In *Artificial intelligence and mathematical theory of computation: papers in honour of John McCarthy*. Academic Press Professional Inc., 1991. DOI: 10.1016/B978-0-12-450010-5.50026-8. 129

Uwe Reyle. Dealing with ambiguities by underspecification: Construction, representation and deduction. *Journal of Semantics*, 10(2):123–179, 1993. DOI: 10.1093/jos/10.2.123. 53, 57, 115

Uwe Reyle. On reasoning with ambiguities. In *Proceedings of the 6th Meeting of the Association for Computational Linguistics (ACL)*, pages 1–8, 1995. 115

Yves Schabes and Aravind K. Joshi. An Earley-type parsing algorithm for tree adjoining grammars. In *Proceedings of the 26th Annual Meeting of the Association for Computational Linguistics (ACL)*, pages 258–269, 1988. DOI: 10.3115/982023.982055. 136

Yves Schabes. *Mathematical and Computational Aspects of Lexicalized Grammars*. PhD thesis, University of Pennsylvania, 1990. 39

Manfred Schmidt-Schauß and Gert Smolka. Attributive concept descriptions with complements. *Artificial Intelligence*, 48(1):1–26, 1991. DOI: 10.1016/0004-3702(91)90078-X. 24

Murray Shanahan, editor. *The Event Calculus Explained*, volume 1600 of *Lecture Notes in Artificial Intelligence (LNAI)*. Springer, 1999. 129

Mark Steedman. Dynamic semantics for tense and aspect. In *Proceedings of the International Joint Conference on Artificial Intelligence (IJCAI)*, pages 1292–1298, 1995. 129

Mark Steedman. *Surface structure and interpretation*. MIT Press, 1996. 57

Rudi Studer, V. Richard Benjamins, and Dieter Fensel. Knowledge engineering: Principles and methods. *Data Knowledge Engineering*, 25(1–2):161–197, 1998. DOI: 10.1016/S0169-023X(97)00056-6. 17

Christoph Tempich, Elena Paslaru Bontas Simperl, Markus Luczak, Rudi Studer, and Helena Sofia Pinto. Argumentation-based ontology engineering. *IEEE Intelligent Systems*, 22 (6):52–59, 2007. DOI: 10.1109/MIS.2007.103. 32

Tania Tudorache, Csongor Nyulas, Natalya Fridman Noy, and Mark A. Musen. Webprotégé: A collaborative ontology editor and knowledge acquisition tool for the web. *Semantic Web*, 4(1): 89–99, 2013. 32

Christina Unger and Philipp Cimiano. Representing and resolving ambiguities in ontology-based question answering. In *Proceedings of the Workshop on Textual Entailment (TextInfer)*, 2011a. 110

Christina Unger and Philipp Cimiano. Pythia: Compositional meaning construction for ontology-based question answering on the semantic web. In *Proceedings of the 16th International Conference on Applications of Natural Language to Information Systems (NLDB)*, volume 6717 of *LNCS*, pages 153–160. Springer, 2011b. DOI: 10.1007/978-3-642-22327-3_15. 140

Christina Unger, Lorenz Bühmann, Jens Lehmann, Axel Ngonga Ngomo, Daniel Gerber, and Philipp Cimiano. Template-based question answering over RDF data. In *Proceedings of the 21st international conference on World Wide Web (WWW)*, pages 639–648, 2012. DOI: 10.1145/2187836.2187923. 140

Michael Uschold and Martin King. Towards a methodology for building ontologies. In *Proceedings of the IJCAI Workshop on Basic Ontological Issues in Knowledge Sharing*, 1995. 32

Michael Uschold. Building ontologies: Towards a unified methodology. In *Proceedings of the 16th Annual Conference of the British Computer Society Specialist Group on Expert Systems*, 1996. 17, 32

Naushad UzZaman and James F. Allen. Extracting events and temporal expressions from text. In *Proceedings of the 4th IEEE International Conference on Semantic Computing (ICSC)*, pages 1–8, 2010. DOI: 10.1142/S1793351X10001097. 129

Jan van Eijck and Hans Kamp. Representing discourse in context. Technical report, Centre for Mathematics and Computer Science (CWI), Amsterdam, The Netherlands, 1996. 57

Jan van Eijck and Christina Unger. *Computational Semantics with Functional Programming*. Cambridge University Press, 2010. DOI: 10.1017/CBO9780511778377. 57

Jan van Eijck and Albert Visser. Dynamic semantics. In Edward N. Zalta, editor, *Stanford Encyclopedia of Philosophy*. Winter 2012 edition, 2012. 42, 57

Josef van Genabith and Richard Crouch. Dynamic and underspecified semantics for LFG. In Mary Dalrymple, editor, *Semantics and Syntax in Lexical Functional Grammar: The Resource Logic Approach*. MIT Press, 1999. 57

Boris Villazón-Terrazas, María del Carmen Suárez-Figueroa, and Asunción Gómez-Pérez. A pattern-based method for re-engineering non-ontological resources into ontologies. *International Journal On Semantic Web and Information Systems*, 6(4):27–63, 2010. DOI: 10.4018/jswis.2010100102. 32

Sebastian Walter, Christina Unger, and Philipp Cimiano. A corpus-based approach for the induction of ontology lexica. In *Proceedings of the 18th International Conference on Application of Natural Language to Information Systems (NLDB)*, 2013. DOI: 10.1007/978-3-642-38824-8_9. 4

Menzo Windhouwer and Sue Ellen Wright. Linking to linguistic data categories in isocat. In *Linked Data in Linguistics*, pages 99–107. Springer, 2012. DOI: 10.1007/978-3-642-28249-2_10. 66

Yuk Wah Wong and Raymond J. Mooney. Learning synchronous grammars for semantic parsing with lambda calculus. In *Proceedings of the 45th Annual Meeting of the Association for Computational Linguistics (ACL)*, 2007. 7

XTAG Research Group. A Lexicalized Tree Adjoining Grammar for English. Technical Report IRCS-01-03, University of Pennsylvania, 2001. URL http://www.cis.upenn.edu/~xtag/tech-report/. 94

Ichiro Yamada, Kentaro Torisawa, Jun'ichi Kazama, Kow Kuroda, Masaki Murata, Stijn De Saeger, Francis Bond, and Asuka Sumida. Hypernym discovery based on distributional similarity and hierarchical structures. In *Proceedings of the International Conference on Empirical Methods in Natural Language Processing (EMNLP)*, pages 929–937, 2009. 7

Luke S. Zettlemoyer and Michael Collins. Learning to map sentences to logical form: Structured classification with probabilistic categorial grammars. In *Proceedings of the 21st Conference in Uncertainty in Artificial Intelligence (UAI)*, pages 658–666, 2005. 7

Authors' Biographies

PHILIPP CIMIANO

Philipp Cimiano is professor of computer science at Bielefeld University and head of the Semantic Computing group, affiliated with the Cluster of Excellence on Cognitive Interaction Technology (CITEC). He received his doctoral degree in applied computer science from the University of Karlsruhe (now KIT) on the topic of learning ontologies from text. He has a wide range of publications in the areas of natural language processing, ontology learning, knowledge acquisition and representation, and the Semantic Web. He was nominated one of *AI's 10 to Watch* by the *IEEE Intelligent Systems Magazine* in 2008, an award given to the top 10 young researchers in the field of artificial intelligence worldwide.

CHRISTINA UNGER

Christina Unger is a postdoctoral researcher in the Semantic Computing group affiliated with the Cluster of Excellence on Cognitive Interaction Technology (CITEC) at Bielefeld University. She received her Ph.D. from the Utrecht Institute of Linguistics (UiL-OTS), the Netherlands, in 2010, on the topic of the relationship between syntactic displacement and semantic scope. Her major research interest lies in the area of computational semantics, with a focus on ontology-based natural language understanding, question answering, and the automatic generation of grammars from the lexicon-ontology interface. In her spare time, she follows the ups and downs of the local soccer club, Arminia Bielefeld.

JOHN McCRAE

John McCrae is a postdoctoral researcher in the Semantic Computing group affiliated with the Cluster of Excellence on Cognitive Interaction Technology (CITEC) at Bielefeld University. He received an MSci in mathematics and computer science from Imperial College London, UK in 2006. In 2009, he received his Ph.D. from the National Institute of Informatics in Tokyo on the topic of learning consistent ontologies by information extraction. He was a principal investigator and work package leader in the EC-funded project Monnet and is one of the main developers of the ontology-lexicon model *lemon*, now being further advanced under the frame of the W3C Ontology-Lexica Community Group.